STOIC
IN LOVE

45 MODERN RULES

*Ancient wisdom to make dating,
domestic boredom and break-ups
a bit less terrible*

ANNIE LAWSON
with illustrations by Oslo Davis

murdoch books
Sydney | London

CONTENTS

PART THREE ~ BREAKING UP

To Henry and Finny, my two loves, to Yoshi and Boo, who are not far behind, to Mum and Dad for enveloping me with love, to Anthony for his generous endorsement, and to Dunstan for his significant contribution to this book.

INTRODUCTION

IT IS BAFFLING that we emerged from the primordial soup in an indifferent cosmos to create music, maths and M&M's, our atoms tracing back to the fiery cauldrons of dying stars. Chemistry and coincidence have given us laughter, suffering, boredom and love. Central to the human condition, love inspired the Taj Mahal, *Romeo and Juliet* and Kiss's 'I Was Made for Lovin' You'. Love can be kind, sweet, tolerable, funny, gentle, fickle and fleeting. But also complex, draining, scary, demanding, difficult and unpredictable. What does love even mean? Why is it so messy, and how do we avoid mistaking it for neediness, dependency or lust?

'Love is the one thing we are capable of perceiving that transcends dimensions of time and space,' Anne Hathaway's character in *Interstellar* says. Some say this line is twee, but she has a point – love ignores physics. The Hindu mystic poet and Krishna devotee Mirabai spoke about the spark of love that lights the cosmos, which 'will bring all the madness you need to unfurl yourself across the universe'. Shakespeare famously cautioned that 'the course of true love never did run smooth'. And when love is broken, 'sorrow abides and happiness takes his leave'.

It remains a mystery whether love comes from some spiritual force, from deep within our brains or from some energy field created when we meet our other half. Maybe it's the result of a cocktail of hormones, or just serendipity. Or maybe it is as simple as a shared passion for beer, badminton or bridge. Some say love does not really exist at all – that it is merely a human construct designed to connect and enslave us in order to propagate the human species. Either way, finding the right kind of love is like winning Lotto, which may explain why we crave it so acutely. It is much easier, of course, to find the wrong kind of love. Relationships do not need a significant betrayal to enter choppy waters.

Love requires patience, curiosity and acceptance of an unknowable future – the very virtues the Stoic philosophers embodied. How do we navigate love's life cycles, from the search for a soulmate to spicing up a stale relationship to surviving heartache when things don't work out? There is nothing lovelier than being in love, but how do you keep the cockles of your heart nice and toasty when things turn sour? The Stoics can help with that.

What would I know about love? My crushes include Simon Le Bon, Bono, George Michael, the construction worker from the Village People, and Caitlyn Jenner when she was Bruce and played a lawyer called Ron in the Village People movie *Can't Stop the Music*. I've had dalliances and dates with a camera operator, a policeman, a politician, a nightclub bouncer, a comedian with a mullet, an artist, various media/journalism people and a South African man who looked and sounded like Cliff Richard. I've also counselled many friends along the way as they negotiated singledom, dating, early and long-term love, and of course break-ups.

All this taught me that the key to a good relationship is not only having someone who amuses you, regular visits to a nice holiday resort and lots of storage (to avoid fights over clutter), but also finding a partner to do nothing with. When I asked others the secret to a loving relationship, their answers varied from finding the right person to expecting only 80 per cent of your needs to be met, plus making lots of teas and coffees for your partner. We all have different thresholds for what makes a good pairing. For some it means excitement and electricity, for others comfort and predictability. Love is about change – a concept that, the Stoics said, inevitably involves losing something but gaining something new.

I first waded into the world of online dating in May 2003. It was early days for internet dating, but it would be the first and last time I searched for love virtually. I matched with a man called Doug, who worked in television as a director. His profile picture was blurry and obscured by a camera. I hoped this date might end a horror stretch of bad liaisons. I was wrong.

Two hours before we were to meet at a club in Soho, London, Doug sent me a flurry of messages: 'You have a magical presence' (we hadn't met yet), 'you have such a great personality' (we'd only ever texted) and 'I like your whimsical turn of phrase' (my answers had been mostly yes or no). Already I could sense there was little chance this man would be the love of my life. I suggested a communications blackout before our date to build a bit of excitement. He agreed and complimented me on being so clever.

In real life, he looked like a younger Donald Trump. When he said hi, he sounded like a younger Donald Trump. We ordered drinks and the conversation shifted to films. I told Doug I loved *Star Wars*. He moved in closer, his brown cords pressed to my jeans, and twirled a lock of my hair before sniffing it. I flinched. As he retreated, he mumbled something about having never yet met a woman who liked *Star Wars*.

I went to the bathroom and texted my mate Lizzy. 'Help! I'm trapped on a date from hell with a creepy hair sniffer!' A few minutes passed ... nothing. I called to ask why she hadn't responded to my text. 'What text?' she said.

When I inspected my messages again, I felt as though my organs might shut down. I had texted Doug, not Lizzy. My options were to stay in the bathroom until he left, face the music or fake my own death.

If I'd known anything about Stoic wisdom from 2000 years ago, I might have focused instead on what I could control and not worried

Introduction

too much about what I could not. The Stoic philosopher Epictetus said: 'It's not what happens to you but how you react that matters.' If he could endure being enslaved by a cruel master who deliberately broke his leg, then surely I could manage a misdirected text to a Donald Trump doppelganger?

The Stoics believed it is not the thing itself that disturb us, but our interpretation of its significance. When a date goes badly wrong or you are ghosted, you can choose how you respond. That much is within your power.

I walked out of the bathroom to see a grim-faced Doug, who said, 'I'm off.' At least he was right about that.

How can Stoicism help?

In a world of complex and contradictory dating and relationship advice, the practical insights from two millennia ago can provide us with a framework for finding, keeping and getting over love. In *Latin Love Lessons*, author Charlotte Higgins said the Romans had a great deal to teach us about love. The Rome of the love poems she dissects did not differ too much from our current times in how its people sought fleeting pleasures. Stoicism offers plenty of useful advice on managing the euphoric highs and crushing lows of dating, long-term relationships and life-changing bust-ups. Rather than end a relationship when someone becomes too annoying, or remain in a substandard one, Stoicism can help us focus on what matters, encouraging us to consider our response before reacting and thus to make better decisions.

Stoic philosophy was founded in Greece by Zeno, a wealthy merchant who, after being shipwrecked on a voyage in around 304 BCE, went to Athens, where he studied and developed his thinking. The Stoic virtues of courage, temperance, patience and justice can help us manage tricky relationships. The central themes are to differentiate between what we can and cannot control, to not waste time worrying about things we can't change, to pause before reacting and to take action when confronted with difficulty.

Seneca the Younger was a Stoic philosopher whose romantic life was far from straightforward. In 41 CE, he was exiled to Corsica for eight years after he was dubiously accused by the empress Messalina of adultery with the emperor's niece Julia Livilla. Later in life he was married to a younger woman, Pompeia Paulina. In 49 CE, Seneca was recalled to Rome, where he became the tutor of the new empress Agrippina's son, the future emperor Nero.

Seneca believed that destructive passions, especially anger and grief, must be uprooted or moderated according to reason.

He said that 'love in its essence is spiritual fire' that could ignite and transform us on a deeper level. Love was not a fleeting emotion: its spiritual nature possessed a powerful and transcendent energy that connected us to the divine, dispelled darkness and healed wounds. For Seneca, love could encourage self-discovery and fuel passion within us. It expanded our capacity for empathy, compassion and understanding, reinforcing that we are all interconnected.

Stoic in Love uses the ancient wisdom of Stoic philosophy to help us find romantic love, build and nurture our relationships, and determine whether to stay or go when things become too predictable or go pear-shaped. With practical wisdom on how to navigate the world of dating, insights on making relationships better and more enduring, and strategies for breaking up well, this book reminds us that the world is all about change. So let's emulate the Stoics and focus on things we can control, like our thoughts, behaviours and actions. And worry less about a date who compulsively talks about the mating habits of goannas, a partner's habit of littering the house with singular dirty socks, or an ex who one-ups you on their superior parenting – for these give our life its colour, and teach us what we want and don't want from love.

Introduction

PART ONE
DATING

'Courtship is to marriage, as a very witty
prologue to a very dull play.'
William Congreve, *The Old Bachelor*

DOs & DON'Ts

LISTEN TO: 'A Wink and a Smile', Harry Connick Jr; 'I Believe in a Thing
Called Love', The Darkness; 'Beautiful Stranger', Madonna
DON'T LISTEN TO: 'You're Nobody 'Til Somebody Loves You', Dean Martin;
'Tired of Being Alone', Al Green; 'Oh No Not You Again', Australian Crawl
EAT: Anything that does not lodge in your teeth (i.e. not parsley) or splatter
your top
DON'T EAT: Osso buco, spaghetti bolognese, tabbouleh salad, garlic,
curried sausages
DRINK: Pretty much anything (in moderation), except ...
DON'T DRINK: Sex on the Beach cocktail, rocket fuel shots or red wine
(to avoid crimson teeth)
WATCH: *Before Sunrise*
DON'T WATCH: *The 40-Year-Old Virgin*; *Bridesmaids*
READ: *How to Not Die Alone* by Logan Ury; *Love Stories* by Trent Dalton
DON'T READ: *Act Like a Lady, Think Like a Man* by Steve Harvey

The path to love is strewn with swipes in the wrong direction, unanswered texts, declarations of love followed by silence, and disappointment when someone claims to be 30 and then turns up to a date looking like Dumbledore.

With serendipity increasingly taking a back seat, we must embrace the virtual possibilities of love and tackle it as we would a profession, setting goals and strategic plans, carefully managing an array of difficult stakeholders and holding meetings (i.e. dates) with actionable outcomes (i.e. anything from never seeing them again to a bit of romance on the side to marriage and babies). As you navigate ghosting, breadcrumbing and gaslighting, remember that the right person for you should not be hard work, and preferably should elevate your spirit after you spend time with them.

But one person's coveted attribute is another's red flag. Some people might not mind a date with someone with golden retriever earlobes who gnaws at a bowl of nuts like a squirrel and scrapes the plate with their spoon. That would be purgatory for others. Remaining indifferent to the outcome of a date is the perfect Stoic mindset to adopt as you navigate the dating minefield.

Complaining about the lack of love prospects and sitting around fruitlessly waiting for love to find you may not help your cause. It's time to get to work.

RULE 1
Give love a chance

'Love can create universes.
Love and wisdom are equal.'

Agni Yoga, *Leaves of Morya's Garden*

YOU NEED LOOK no further than the TV franchises *Love Is Blind* and
Married at First Sight, where people get engaged or marry on their first
date, to see that there are many – often dubious – paths to love. Finding
love is a bit like Frodo's quest in *The Lord of the Rings*, as there are plenty
of virtual and real-life orcs, Gollums and Sarumans. The idea is to find
a Gandalf, an Arwen or an Aragorn (yes, please).

Gone are the serendipitous hook-ups and authentic connections
we made in the workplace, or through friends of friends, or randomly
in a queue for a kebab. Relationships that blossom from our phones
are prefaced by a flurry of texting. As journalist Elle Hunt noted, every
stage of the dating and relationship life cycle can now be conducted
virtually – 'from early butterflies, to getting to know each other, to one
or the other pulling away, to our eventual break-up'.

Matching, messaging and eventually meeting is like an unfulfilling
second job for which you never get paid. Sometimes the message
thread goes quiet just before a meet-up, signalling that your future
spouse has lost interest and found another match. Some people are

brutal and include instructions on their profile such as 'swipe left if you have thin lips', helpfully giving scrollers a strong signpost of dickheadery. Decoding the hidden meaning behind texts that are seen but not responded to is exhausting.

People who use dating apps hate them because of the administrative and spiritual toll. Even people who do not use dating apps hate them. But they have removed social and geographical boundaries, and dramatically widened our pool of prospective partners. The trick is to distinguish between a potential love match, a complete psychopath and a bot. (Though at least you never have to live with the bot and argue over whose turn it is to stack the dishwasher.)

Dating apps try to be helpful by suggesting potential matches, which is fine until they throw up your best friend's husband or your uncle. We all look for certain attributes in people that are non-negotiable. No criminal record, nice breath and well-plucked nasal hair. But look out for any misrepresentation – the kind who photoshops out his double chin and man boobs, or poses with a labrador even though he dislikes dogs. I am not likely to post the photo that shows my own double chin, an unhealthy amount of gum and bird's-nest hair.

Once you do meet in the real world, how can you tell if someone likes you? And when is it appropriate to deploy a playful tap on the arm to initiate a frisson-charged exchange? How do you read the right signals to gauge interest? Flirting builds excitement but does not necessarily culminate in romance.

Apparently, we mirror the gestures of others we are attracted to. According to the BBC, it takes between 90 seconds and four minutes for us to determine whether we find someone attractive. Some 55 per cent of messages signalling attraction come through body language, 38 per cent through the tone and speed of our voice, and 7 per cent from conversation. Playing hard to get apparently does not work, but we like people who are easy for us to get but tricky for others.

What do the Stoics say?

Ancient dating algorithms openly favoured sibling matches. The Roman census during the first to the third centuries CE indicated that more than 16 per cent of documented marriages had some degree of kinship. While not all were perhaps biological brothers and sisters, avoiding siblings on dates was clearly not easy.

In the modern dating world, there is a much wider pool of non-relatives to choose from. Where do we begin? Embracing the Stoic virtues of courage, patience, temperance and justice is a good start. Unfortunately, dating apps do not make a feature of these virtues. The incessant scrolling and targeted algorithms measure success not through a love connection but how long people spend on the apps. This means the desired outcome is for users to have a relationship with technology that lasts longer than any romantic liaison. The focus is on what we are lacking rather than what we have.

Seneca said that instead of wallowing in the absence of love, we should take charge of our own happiness. That means adopting an indifferent mindset to dating outcomes, and not anticipating too much. '[I]f day and night your soul keeps its even and unswerving course, upright and content with itself,' he wrote, 'then you have attained to the greatest good that mortals can possess.'

Of course, this is unrealistic, but it is something to strive towards.

A FINAL WORD FROM THE STOICS

'But having determined in your mind that every thing which shall turn out [result] is indifferent, and does not concern you, and whatever it may be, for it will be in your power to use it well.'
Epictetus, *Discourses*

RULE 2
Do your due diligence

'Diligence is the mother of good fortune, and idleness,
its opposite, never led to good intention's goal.'

Miguel de Cervantes, *Don Quixote*

FOR SOME, a shared love of beer or just being available is enough to convince them that a person is the one. These are woefully insufficient foundations for a life together. That's why the importance of doing your due diligence before a date – or at worst before a relationship and a marriage – cannot be overstated.

Due diligence is about maintaining your standards. Fortunately, the system of dating various people helps us screen out unsuitable connections, mismatches, complete freaks and people who like coriander and offal. But it is not foolproof.

Katherine went out with Steve for several months and failed to heed an early red flag: his glasses were not prescription but plain glass. But she stayed with him – until she found out he was also sleeping with several blokes. The glasses revealed a deceptive side.

Nicky went out with a man known as Dumping Dave. His nickname did not deter her, though, because she felt she could defy his pattern of dumping women after just a few dates. Anyway, after a few dates, he dumped her. Some months later, he contacted her and asked her for a photo of him she took while they were seeing one another. Could she upload the picture to his dating profile to help attract a few women he was texting, he asked her. Sure, she said, and requested his password to access his dating profile. She uploaded the photo and then, as a parting gift, changed his preference from 'man seeking woman' to 'man seeking man'. She didn't hear from him again.

Consideration must also be given to beer goggles and time of night. That man you wouldn't cross the road for at lunchtime seems like an Adonis at midnight. Too often people conduct their due diligence the next morning, when their heads are delicate from too much booze and regret.

You can do your due diligence even when you're on your way to a one-night stand. Gordon and Ryan met Lindsay and Lara at a party, and the women invited the blokes back to the flat they shared. But in the taxi the men overheard the girls chatting about how they thought Donald Trump was a good guy, and they quickly changed their minds: both of them jumped out at the next traffic lights and escaped. This is an example of excellent and timely due diligence.

Significantly more due diligence is required for a lifelong union. Britney Spears both was reckless and then did a U-turn and quickly enforced due diligence in her 2004 marriage in Las Vegas, which lasted all of 55 hours. At least she had the good sense to swiftly pull the plug when it became apparent her childhood friend was no long-term love.

When the actor Rupert Pole met the author Anaïs Nin at a cocktail party, he forgot to ask if she was single – a basic question in any due diligence assessment. They got together, moved to the West Coast of the United States and tied the knot. However, Anaïs frequently flew back to the east coast, purportedly to meet with her publishers. What she failed to disclose was that it was, in fact, to spend time with her other husband, a banker.

What do the Stoics say?

When making decisions, the Stoics first looked at whether a situation is within your control. And vetting a date is squarely under your control. But their behaviour, actions, personality and tendency to blurt out bad jokes or ghost you are not things you can control.

Epictetus would not have cracked onto someone in a kebab queue after a night at the pub. 'When you imagine some pleasure, beware that it does not carry you away, like other imaginations,' he said. 'Next remember two things: how long you will enjoy the pleasure, and also how long you will afterwards repent and revile yourself.'

Think through the consequences before you deploy a terrible pick-up line to an unsuitable stranger or — worse — have a one-night stand with them and discover their extensive machete collection.

The Stoics were not slaves to their passions, valuing temperance and resistance to unbridled lust or greed. Seneca believed true happiness could be found in enjoyment of the present 'without any anxious dependence upon the future'. He advised not to 'amuse ourselves with either hopes or fears but to rest satisfied with what we have, which is abundantly sufficient'.

So be happy with what you've got. And don't rush into a relationship because of societal pressure or a fear of ending up on the shelf. It can take that final Stoic virtue, courage, to be honest with yourself about what is best for you.

A FINAL WORD FROM THE STOICS

'The great blessings of mankind are within us and within our reach. A wise man is content with his lot, whatever it may be, without wishing for what he has not.'

Seneca, 'On a Happy Life'

RULE 2 Do your due diligence

RULE 3
Expect a dating horror story

> 'How much worse can it get than finishing dinner,
> having him reach over, pull a hair out of my head,
> and start flossing with it at the table?'
>
> Meg Ryan in *When Harry Met Sally*

THERE CAN BE competition among friends about who's had the worst date, but Meg Ryan's character in *When Harry Met Sally* arguably has the winner. Unless you're one of those people who met the love of their lives early and has remained blissfully happy ever since (no one likes those people), then you most likely have a dating horror story or two (or 11). The horror starts well before the date, when a married family friend at a gathering asks in front of everyone why you are still single and whether it's because you are asexual. You say curtly that you are not, and then ask in front of his wife whether he is hung like a twig. Everyone looks at you with pity, because not only are you a desperate single, you are an angry desperate single.

To prove to my family friends that I was not asexual, I agreed to be set up on a blind date. A friend, Maxine, invited me to a dinner party. My date's name was Scottie. Maxine assured me he was great, yet said, rather ominously, 'Either he'll stalk you or you'll never hear from him again.' It turned out Scottie looked like Boris Johnson and wore a blue striped shirt, a watermelon tie and a gold-buttoned navy blazer, with chinos and beige Velcro shoes.

We sat down for dinner and merrily discussed politics, life and the universe. 'Don't you think the House of Lords needs reforming so it's more democratic?' I said, a bit too stridently. 'Don't you think the whole peerage and class issue is a disgrace?' With each statement, I stabbed the air with my fork. I failed to notice that Scottie had disappeared, perhaps to avoid being impaled by a utensil. The host eventually found him hiding in a cupboard, a sign that he should be put in the 'you'll never hear from him again' bucket.

Ricky Gervais' character David Brent in *The Office* was unable to conceal his disappointment with online dating. 'I don't know what to expect, to be honest,' he told the camera. 'I haven't been impressed so far. Erm, I hope they're vetting them, because the computer seems to be throwing up any old rubbish.' When his date eventually showed up and he thought she was a random person, he said to her, 'Yeah, I was expecting a blind date, and was worried you were it.' Brent's visceral disappointment was probably shared by the other women he had dated.

Miranda Hart, in her eponymous show, went on a blind date with an army doctor. His nickname was Dreamboat Charlie, named after a floating brothel, and he asked if she wanted the short or long version of how the name came about. She requested the short version, before throwing a glass of red wine over herself in an attempt to bring the evening to an end.

These vignettes remind us that the search for love requires patience and realistic expectations of some unsuitable matches in our search for love. Fear that someone better is around the corner can sabotage a good enough date. Rom-coms, love songs and romance novels would have you believe that it's a breeze to find the person of your dreams. But we are complex beings with a unique mix of genes, experiences and intolerances. A date who uses an exaggerated French accent for words like croissant, patisserie or enchanté, or someone who wears a jacket but fails to put their arms in the sleeves is game over for me.

The road to romance is paved with disappointment. But each horror date builds our resilience by teaching us more about what we don't want, and focuses our attention on qualities in others that better complement our personality. They also make excellent conversational fodder on the next date – assuming that too does not take a turn for the worse.

What do the Stoics say?

Praemeditatio malorum is a technique of imagining the worst-case scenario in order to prepare for a negative event. Roman emperor Marcus Aurelius used this psychological tactic to better regulate his emotions when confronted with life's difficulties. He was a fan of Epictetus, invoking his dichotomy of control to face obstacles. Epictetus said: 'The chief task in life is simply this: to identify and separate matters so that I can say clearly to myself which are externals not under my control, and which have to do with the choices I actually control. Where then do I look for good and evil? Not to uncontrollable externals, but within myself to the choices that are my own.'

As it turns out, we control very little – not what happens to us, nor what people say or do. How we think and the judgements we make about people and events are under our control. So we must take ownership of our thoughts, actions and responses to situations. When things happen that are out of their control, the Stoic lets go of them. If we anticipate that there's a certain percentage of the population who will displease us, then we can stay a step ahead and remain unbothered.

A FINAL WORD FROM THE STOICS

'Not to feel exasperated, or defeated, or despondent because your days aren't packed with wise and moral actions. But to get back up when you fail, to celebrate behaving like a human – however imperfectly – and fully embrace the pursuit that you've embarked on.'
Marcus Aurelius, *Meditations*

RULE 3 Expect a dating horror story

RULE 4
Beware red flags

'Of all forms of caution, caution in love is perhaps the most fatal to true happiness.'
Bertrand Russell, *The Conquest of Happiness*

ONE OF THE best ways to test the humanity of a date is to observe how they treat the waiting staff. If they're rude, then it's best to say you forgot you had a dentist appointment. Another red flag is if the Xs that were once liberally used after messages slow to a trickle, before disappearing altogether. There are also green flags, which are positive, and beige flags, which signal an odd trait, such as slurping a drink, that's not a deal breaker but something to watch. Look for clues in online profile photos – a bunch of dusty fabric flowers in the background, or a quadbike, or a MAGA hat.

A date who makes you feel inadequate or enquires about your sanity is to be avoided. 'Gaslighting' gained momentum in 1944 with the movie *Gaslight*, about an international criminal who married his wife for her jewels, but made her believe she was losing her grip on reality. Gaslighting is a blazing red flag for psychological manipulation and oppression.

Someone exploring red flags put this question into the Facebook ether: 'What makes someone instantly unattractive?' The responses varied from liar, disrespectful, angry, entitlement, selfishness, narcissism, superiority, sweary, unempathetic, player, arrogant, being drunk, racism, bullying, pettiness, bad manners, judgemental, being a dictator, greed, mean-spirited, stingy, or cruel (including to animals). It was a long list of odious qualities, from people who requested nudes to those who talked to someone else while you were on the phone with them. For one friend of mine it was the way a guy held his hand flush against his steering wheel.

Some took umbrage to prospective dates who chewed gum with their mouth open, a large ego, a lack of kindness, or being hoity-toity or fake. Materialism, jealousy and sneakiness were equally unattractive qualities. Gigantic earlobes were apparently a turn-off (bad news for those like me with golden retriever–like lobes). And evil eyes were not regarded as appealing. Bad grammar and picking your nose were noted as being unsavoury in a prospective love interest, although some may argue the latter is much worse.

Valid reasons to quit a date: bad teeth, snobbery, a lack of humility, dishonesty, being demanding, unfaithful or conceited, humourlessness, face tattoos and singlets with huge armholes. Overall, using profanities, animal cruelty and being disrespectful rated the most mentions. The quality that was voted most unattractive was anyone who 'answered these stupid online questions'. Fair enough.

Psychotherapist and author Philippa Perry advised one reader who felt a 'punch in the gut' each time her date ogled other women to explain that this behaviour made her feel inadequate, unlovable, insecure and vulnerable. If the partner gave 'preferential treatment to his own feelings' by failing to amend his behaviour, then she might 'consider being with someone who brings out the best in you rather than your insecurities'.

These days, there's also the question of whether your online date is really a human at all. As AI improves and bots become more sophisticated, they are being weaponised by scammers to extract cash from vulnerable people looking for love.

But one person's red flag might be another's soulmate. A woman in Canada described herself as an 'ecosexual' and was in an 'erotic' relationship with an oak tree, according to the *Daily Mail*. Then there was the bride-to-be who was engaged to a ghost. She didn't have a ring as her fiancé was picky and she didn't want to scare him off, but she hoped they would have babies. In 2009 a Japanese man became the first to marry a virtual girlfriend from the Nintendo game *Love Plus*. He surely won't be the last.

What do the Stoics say?

Marcus Aurelius advised that rather than focusing on the flaws of others, we should remember that we too are flawed. He also prepared himself to deal with disappointment by expecting to encounter people with unsavoury traits: 'All these things happen to them by reason of their ignorance of what is good and evil … I can neither be injured by any of them, for no one can fix on me what is ugly, nor can I be angry with my kinsman, nor hate him.'

Epictetus reminds us that it's our own feelings that are the true source of our troubles. Finger pointing is futile, and the impulse to blame others foolish. We make moral progress only when we cease blaming others for our misfortune, because our own response to disturbances is what causes us discomfort. Examining our own attitudes helps us avoid giving a stormy emotional response to an unhappy turn of events.

A FINAL WORD FROM THE STOICS
'If anyone tells you that such a person speaks ill of you, don't make excuses about what is said of you, but answer: "He does not know my other faults, else he would not have mentioned only these."'
Epictetus, *Enchiridion*

RULE 5
Don't get too drunk

**'First you take a drink,
then the drink takes a drink,
then the drink takes you.'**
Attributed to F. Scott Fitzgerald

ONE FATEFUL NIGHT at an exclusive club where high-society
weddings and events were usually held, I experienced the greatest
humiliation of my life. A family friend's daughter was marrying
a doctor, and they invited 200 people to a no-expenses-spared
reception. I was seated on the table reserved for singles and misfits
while everyone else was coupled up. I responded to the humiliation
by drinking a vat of wine.

Towards the end of the evening, we formed a circle so the bride
and groom could thank us individually before heading off to the
honeymoon suite. But I drunkenly railed against the tradition – and
the whole marital institution – and yelled out to the group: 'I hate
husbands, I hate wives!' The guests looked at me agog.

My mother ushered me out of the venue and ticked me off for
drinking too much. I begged her to let me buy a hot dog on the way
home, so we stopped at a 24-hour convenience store. I found the hot
dog but could not get it into the paper bag. The man behind the counter
said: 'That's a bag for pies, not hot dogs.' I turned to him and said:

'I'll put my hot dog into any fucken' bag I want.' This low point followed a three-year stretch of singledom.

My mother held an 'apology' dinner party, where I had to stand up and issue a formal apology to the bride and groom and their families. The convenience store bloke could not be located. The whole experience taught me that I should not drink two litres of wine when I am in a singles slump.

A few weeks later, having not learned the lesson, I had a date with a comedian. He had a black mullet and a parachute bomber jacket. Despite the unusual hair, he was a deep-thinking introvert who looked uncomfortable at being set up on a blind date. I consulted a friend who was also a comedian about what I should talk about. He advised me to play it cool, be amusing and don't get drunk.

I did none of these things. When I arrived, he was friendly but he had a fixed smile each time I spoke. At one point, the pocket on my trousers became ensnared on the corner of the table as I sat down and ripped slightly, revealing a glimpse of my purple granny underwear. I was rattled and guzzled a carafe of wine; he sipped a beer with a look of disapproval. We both ate our meals with remarkable efficiency, said our farewells and never crossed paths again.

What do the Stoics say?

Marcus Aurelius had two influential people in his life who shaped his attitude to alcohol. His adoptive father, the emperor Antoninus Pius, was 'able both to abstain from, and to enjoy, those things which many are too weak to abstain from, and cannot enjoy without excess'. Antoninus's ability to refrain was 'the mark of a man who has a perfect and invincible soul', and made the rest of us who get sozzled on dates look bad.

In contrast, Marcus's adoptive brother, Lucius Verus, was an infamous hedonist, a gambler who plied the brothels and taverns of Rome. Marcus was fond of him but, in a typically Stoic way, was grateful for his own vigilance over his own moral character. The Stoics, unsurprisingly, drank in moderation but considered alcoholism as a disease. Seneca viewed drunkenness as a 'single hour of hilarious madness' followed by a 'sickness of many days' and the cause of 'great mental disquietude'. Temperance was an important virtue, he wrote. Excess in everything was discouraged, meaning a light tipple was just fine, but abstinence for the wrong reasons was also frowned upon.

In his Discourses, Epictetus criticised those who boasted about being teetotal. 'If it is good for you to drink, drink; but if not, you are acting ridiculously. But if it is good for you and you do drink, say nothing about it to those who are displeased with water-drinkers. What then, do you wish to please these very men?' Of course, sometimes a tipple can help with the final virtue of courage, when entering the bar to meet a date for the first time, or letting someone know that there is, in fact, no spark.

A FINAL WORD FROM THE STOICS

'When men have wearied themselves with wine and lust, when night fails them before their debauch is done, when the pleasures which they have heaped upon a body that is too small to hold them begin to fester, at such times they utter in their wretchedness those lines of Virgil: Thou knowest how, amid false-glittering joys. We spent that last of nights.'
Seneca, 'On Drunkenness'

RULE 6
Be considerate with location and attire

**'Is she kind as she is fair?
For beauty lives with kindness.'**
William Shakespeare, *Two Gentlemen of Verona*

IT WAS VALENTINE'S DAY in the middle of February on Scotland's Ben Nevis, the highest peak in the British Isles. The day was cold, wet and misty. In her spare time, Elizabeth liked puppies, shopping and pampering. Not ice-laden slopes that freeze your fingers off. However, she liked Gordon enough to spend a romantic afternoon in gale-force winds where life and death hang in the balance as the temperature drops and night falls.

By the time they were nearing the summit, it was shrouded in cloud. Elizabeth was shivering and scared, and reluctantly Gordon suggested they turn back. As they descended a steep path, they worked out it was not a path but a gully. It was dark, visibility was poor and they had no idea where they were. They stayed put and slept in an orange survival bag.

The next day, Gordon asked Elizabeth if they could mount another push for the summit. She gave him a stare icier than the terrain they had negotiated to make it to safety. The relationship continued for a few months until he attempted to take her up Snowdon, the highest peak in Wales, a move that ended things swiftly. Determining earlier that Elizabeth was averse to mountain climbing would have avoided an unnecessary ordeal.

Where to go on a date says a lot about a person. Are they a coffee shop person, or a pub or nightclub aficionado, or are they into glow-in-the-dark golf or posing nude at life drawing classes? Do they want to meet up at a jelly-wrestling competition or in a hotel room on the first date? These are red flags for some people and a welcome deviation from a coffee date for others. Dates are an investment in time, money and energy, so going somewhere free like an art gallery or museum means a minimum outlay if the date ends up a dud. And a good investment if there is a decent return.

Asked her top tip for online dating, Amelia said punctuality was critical. When she met up with her first online date, he was half an hour late, failed to apologise and then spoke only of his fear of death. Not boyfriend material. Not any kind of material.

Even more challenging is matching the location with what to wear. You want to strike that balance between being noncommittal but alluring, aloof but engaged, and attractive but not too try-hard. If the date involves indoor rock climbing, a skirt or culottes are not going to work. The rule of thumb is to make sure you do not have toothpaste smeared on your top and that your underpants are clean. The rest will take care of itself.

What do the Stoics say?

The consideration shown to you by a date can tell you a lot about them as a future partner. Some of us are more independent than others, more open, more willing to try new things. But there can be few who would ask for less rather than more kindness and consideration from another person.

RULE 6 Be considerate with location and attire

Stoics encouraged consideration of others, to put yourself in their shoes when contemplating actions. We are advised to empathise with their struggles, and while we might hope that this kindness will be reciprocated, we shouldn't demand or expect that it is. Dragging a person opposed to hiking up a mountainside in treacherous weather shows a distinct lack of consideration. As Marcus Aurelius puts it, we are born to be kind.

We should not only listen to someone's words, but also seek out and understand their underlying emotions, beliefs and thoughts. Is your date someone who is going to enjoy being surprised by a tandem skydive trip, or will they be happy walking the dog around the same park every week as long as they are with you?

You only have control over your own actions. Don't seek to change the other person – who they are is outside of your control. You must either adapt yourself and accept – maybe even enjoy – the person they are, or move on, as that may be the most considerate path.

A FINAL WORD FROM THE STOICS

'Accustom yourself to give careful attention to what others are saying, and try your best to enter into the mind of the speaker.'

Marcus Aurelius, *Meditations*

RULE 7
Use maths to find the right partner

'Mathematics, rightly viewed, possesses not only truth,
but supreme beauty – a beauty cold and austere,
like that of a sculpture.'

Bertrand Russell, *Philosophical Essays*

SIMON MET HIS HUSBAND, Gary, by applying the '80 per cent rule' to their relationship: be content with 80 per cent of your expectations being met and 20 per cent being unmet. 'If you find somebody you love, the maximum you are going to get is 80 per cent,' Simon says. No person is perfect or pure – they may be a messy blend of kindness and cruelty, joy and sadness, and equanimity and anger. Genuine intimacy is allowing our partners to see us at our weakest. Instead of relying on emotion and instinct, Simon invoked mathematics to keep his expectations of the relationship at a more reasonable and achievable level.

Numbers can be useful when trying to find someone in the first place, too. To maximise the chances of the best outcome, we should forget the first 37 per cent of any options, including prospective partners. Philosophy writer Jonny Thomson has proposed something called the 'optimal stopping problem' to determine how many people you should date before settling down. His approach uses both mathematics and psychology to help us make a decision. Out of 100 options, he proposes, you should try – but not buy – the first 37. The sampling period is useful for identifying what works and what does not. If any subsequent option eclipses your benchmark, then you should go for it.

An example from a dating pool of ten people would be to have fun with the first three but refrain from a second date because better will likely be around the corner. The next-best date after those first three is the one to hold onto.

The trouble is that we are not rational in this way. Emotions render our minds thoroughly irrational. We must wrestle with the explore/exploit trade-off to either pursue a guaranteed win (exploit) or risk an unknown future outcome (explore). According to research published in *Nature Neuroscience*, too much exploring and exploiting are detrimental. It is best to strike a balance.

Numbers are also important when it comes to deciding when to settle down. Friends celebrating their 25th wedding anniversary and 33 years together told me that 22 was the optimum age for them to meet a life partner, which seems young. Yet the unwritten rule is to play the field for a while, and not settle down too early. But what if you pass up the right person?

If in doubt, wait for number four, age 22 and accept 80 per cent compatibility.

What do the Stoics say?

An inscription on Plato's door, probably at the Academy at Athens, said: 'Let no one enter who does not know mathematics.'

As it turns out, maths would be a very useful skill when dating, were it not for love and lust interfering with our logical brain. Even though 'optimal stopping' came well after the time of the Stoics, their philosophy was rooted in logical concepts such that they developed a system of propositional logic under Chrysippus of Soli (279–206 BCE) that has stood the test of time, being visible in the structure of modern-day computer languages. The system sought to remove value judgements from statements so that they would express only what is true.

For instance:

If it is day, it is light;

It is day;

Therefore it is light.

True Stoic logic might apply this logic to a date, thus:

If my date is boring, they will be a poor long-term match;

They are so dull I feel the need to poke toothpicks in my skin to stay awake;

Therefore they are a bad match.

In the Enchiridion, *Epictetus said the nature of evil does not exist — the universe is indifferent to our struggles. Allowing reason to guide our judgement is likely to produce a better result to any challenge.*

And let's face it — dating is a numbers game, so it makes sense that we should invoke a logical approach if we want to secure our desired outcome.

A FINAL WORD FROM THE STOICS

'Reason, however, is surely the governing element in such a matter as this; as reason has made the decision concerning the happy life.'

Seneca, 'On the True God as Attained by Reason'

RULE 8
Manifest love magically

'Love is the magician, the enchanter,
that changes worthless things to Joy,
and makes royal kings and queens
of common clay.'

Robert G. Ingersoll, *Orthodoxy*

AMERICAN ACTOR Colman Domingo met his husband of 19 years during a chance encounter. Domingo related on *The Graham Norton Show* how he went to buy a face mask at a Walgreens in Berkeley, California, in 2005. He saw a guy with long hair and a lip piercing walk out, and they stared at one another for a moment. His future husband seemed to be embroiled in an argument with a woman. The man walked down the street but they looked back at one another, and Domingo waved at the stranger before they went on their separate ways. He considered posting an ad on a 'Missed Connections' site, but noticed an ad that had been posted two hours earlier by his future spouse that said: 'Saw you outside of Walgreens, Berkeley.' Serendipity, magic or karma?

A cynic might dismiss coincidences as just that, rather than lay cosmic patterns over the vast number of interactions we have each day. We are guided by storytelling and pattern recognition. The true story here, though, is that Domingo found someone he loves deeply.

Sometimes we can feel karmically cursed. A detractor at work CCs everyone in an email to highlight an important piece of work you have overlooked. You back into a bollard and dent the car. A tax bill drops that's the size of a house deposit. Your efforts to find love or jump-start a loveless relationship are fruitless. For those ensconced in a relationship, the universe does not always reward smugness (one can only hope).

At a media event, a mid-level television personality flashed her large diamond engagement ring to Kaz, who was raw from a recent break-up. As the champagne flowed, the celebrity dragged her fiancé over to join the conversation. 'I see you don't have a ring,' the TV presenter said, inspecting Kaz's left hand. 'Are you at least in a relationship?' Kaz said no, at which point the celebrity deployed a sympathetic head tilt and pout. She said, in a baby voice, 'There aren't many blokes left like my fiancé. Better hurry up!' Two weeks later, the celebrity's fiancé dumped her.

I visited a psychic after a relationship break-up to see if a new love was on my horizon. Her name was Wanda, and she foresaw a marriage for me in ten years' time, with two children, but cautioned that it would have its ups and downs. I was more worried about the ten-year wait than the rocky patches.

Before this, I was in a long-term relationship with Stephen. We had been living together for four years and there were serious cracks due to mismatched personalities. He arranged his shirts by colour and check pattern, alphabetised his cereal boxes and spent his weekends at classic car shows. My cupboards were jammed with scrunched-up clothes, I left cereal packets half-open on the kitchen bench and spent my weekends at the pub with friends. One afternoon, he announced that he had visited a clairvoyant, who did not see me in his future. Coincidentally, the psychic I had seen also had reservations about the relationship. It is no coincidence that, soon after, we ended things.

A Korean concept called *In-Yun* – explored in the 2023 film *Past Lives* – explores cosmic balance and interconnectedness, teaching us to embrace light and shade in relationships and that our actions have karmic consequences. Joy and sorrow, passion and calm, and unity and individuality are not opposing forces. Accepting that they are complementary and embracing our differences helps us navigate relationships with greater equanimity. Karmic reality reinforces kindness, respect and love in nurturing fulfilling relationships.

What do the Stoics say?

The Stoics believed we must take responsibility for our actions. Even had they known of the Buddhist concept of karma, they would surely not have adopted it, instead focusing on living a virtuous life because it is the right thing to do – for the individual and for those around them. In their worldview, the too-confident TV presenter's downfall came from failing to control her emotions and bragging about her good fortune. Her fiancé's actions were squarely out of her control, though perhaps he would have been more inclined to stay had she bragged less. Nor can there be any judgement on whether that event was intrinsically good or bad, as the universe is indifferent to our struggles.

Seneca wrote of the cruel, fickle mistress that is Fortune: 'harsh and invincible is her power; things deserved and undeserved must we suffer just as she wills ... Like a mistress that is changeable and passionate and neglectful of her slaves, she will be capricious in both her rewards and her punishments. What need is there to weep over parts of life? The whole of it calls for tears.' Whether the tides of our fortune change for good or bad, we must build our own resilience.

A FINAL WORD FROM THE STOICS

'For the soul is more powerful than any sort of Fortune; by its own agency it guides its affairs in either direction, and of its own power it can produce a happy life, or a wretched one.'
Seneca, 'On the Fickleness of Fortune'

RULE 8 Manifest love magically

RULE 9
Ghost at your peril

'A naked thinking heart, that makes no show,
Is to a woman, but a kind of ghost.'
— John Donne, 'The Blossom'

HERE'S A CAUTIONARY tale for any would-be ghosters, those who resort to the all-too-common practice of abruptly ending all communications with a romantic partner or date without explanation.

A man who had ghosted his live-in girlfriend ten years earlier found out she was to become his boss. Had he ghosted her after a few dates, he might have got away with it. But ghosting someone he'd lived with for *three years* was almost impossible to bounce back from.

Ten years ago, recognising that he did not share her desire to settle down, he chose to end their relationship by disappearing without a trace in order to avoid a 'break-up drama'. Now he worked as a teacher at an international school and suddenly discovered that the incoming new director was his ex-partner.

After emailing her to 'discuss the way forward in person', he was summoned to a meeting with the school chair and his ex. The chair proposed a series of measures that might allow them to work together, such as never communicating without a third party present, documenting all meetings, banning him from discussing her with colleagues, and limiting his ability to socialise with other staff.

The man decided to quit, accepting his 'comeuppance'.

Ghosting is one of the most widespread and odious practices in the modern world of dating. Wayne took his date to a winter lights show in the city. As they lay on a grassy hill watching a kaleidoscope of colours projected into the sky, sipping wine and kissing, he wondered if he had met the one. At the end of the evening, they arranged to see each other the next weekend. Only he never heard from her again. Ghosting is a piss-weak way to treat another person, and hints at a decline in our societal obligation to look after our fellow humans. We don't need to pursue a romance with everyone who pursues us, but we can sensitively and politely let them know there's a lack of spark.

When we want to understand why a date has ghosted us, we imagine – even hope – that they've been trapped under a bus or suddenly changed their sexuality. This seems far better than the reality of rejection and the discourtesy of ghosting. Every person on the planet who ghosts another person lacks courage. Even so, we must all set our dating expectations low, to minimise the disappointment of this apparent inevitability. And remember that every ghosting you suffer may just be a bullet dodged.

Being ghosted is a cruel thing to experience. Think of the emotions it causes in the person left in the dark: from disbelief ('They must have been in an accident'), to anger ('How could they do this to me?'), to self-blame ('What did I do wrong?'), and finally to grief.

At the other end of the spectrum is 'anti-ghosting', which simply means being a decent human and letting someone know you do not wish to continue seeing them. In other words, just being polite. It is more difficult than just cutting someone off and disappearing into the night, but the beauty of this approach is that, if the person you reject sends a snarky response, then you can take the high ground, unlike bottom-dwelling ghosters.

Another variant is 'self-ghosting'. This new trend sees people not showing up for themselves. That is, they promise to ditch chocolate (for reasons that defy logic) and then do not. Or they vow to limit alcohol, before getting sozzled three times in one week. Or they commit to developing their side hustle, then never put in the work.

Yet another type is 'soft' or 'slow' ghosting. This is a drawn-out situation where messages are responded to at increasingly longer intervals – at first hours later, then days and weeks. 'Breadcrumb ghosting' or 'haunting' is a complex pattern of keeping someone interested, but not allowing them to feel secure in the relationship. A romantic interest might seem like they have vanished, and yet they still remain in your life, popping up now and then to kindle your interest.

Ignoring someone might be easier than telling them you're not interested, but it lacks courage and humanity. And if they happen to become your boss, you'll wish you really were a ghost.

What do the Stoics say?

If someone ghosts you, the Stoics would say the situation is beyond your control. All you have power over is the quality of your own thoughts and values. Do you freak out, stalk your ghosting ex and harass their family and friends? Or do you take the higher ground and let the immature weasel disappear into the night and waste no further energy on them?

The Stoics valued clear communication and respected reason and judgement, so they'd clearly never ghost someone, let alone someone they were romantically involved with. They recognised that how we regulate our emotions, especially during conflict, is intrinsic to our happiness. Regular self-reflection helps us manage our reactions and how we interact with others. If you are being ghosted, refocus your energies elsewhere.

The key Stoic virtues that ghosters lack are justice and courage. If you feel tempted to ghost someone, try the alternative instead: a straightforward, polite, direct message. If you receive a confronting message in response, then there is no need to be drawn in. If, on the

RULE 9 Ghost at your peril

other hand, it is laziness that causes you to ghost, consider the lack of justice that this entails for someone who has invested at least some time in you.

Marcus Aurelius believed that unhappiness and evil came from ignorance and a lack of clear thought. Unclear communication leads to a blockage in our thoughts and actions. But Marcus was not snarky about others. Politely letting someone down imposes clear boundaries and is a better way to manage their expectations. Be polite, offer a brief explanation of why you are not interested, and then move on.

A FINAL WORD FROM THE STOICS

'Everything has two handles, one by which you can carry it, the other by which you cannot. If your brother wrongs you, do not take it by that handle, the handle of his wrong, for you cannot carry it by that, but rather by the other handle – that he is a brother, brought up with you, and then you will take it by the handle that you can carry by.'

Epictetus, *Enchiridion*

RULE 10
Don't worry about rules

'Conventionality is not morality.'
Charlotte Brontë, *Jane Eyre*

IT WAS A SATURDAY, and an 84-year-old relative, Agnes, invited the family over for lunch with a long-time family friend, Brian, who was 85. Over quiche and salad, we chatted about travel, shared friends and the benefits of retirement, before the conversation shifted to threesomes. Turns out, Agnes and Brian had both separately had unscheduled romantic encounters with married couples.

I grabbed the cheese platter and handed it around, desperately trying to change the subject: 'Weather's not great, is it?' They both ignored me.

'It's not really romantic, more exploratory,' Agnes said.

Brian agreed. He said he found the whole experience 'quite complicated ... You're busy all the time with bits and bumps.'

I nearly choked on a piece of blue cheese.

Had I ever had a threesome, they asked.

No, I had not.

Why not?

Because three is one too many, I said.

If our romantic behaviour can be traced back to our childhood role models, typically our family, what did this mean for me? Would I end up in a throuple?

You need to live and love with no regrets, Agnes and her friend said, before the conversation moved on to hip replacements.

I asked other friends for their views. One said he had dabbled in threesomes in his 20s after two women invited him over for the evening. He said he felt inadequate and unable to keep up, but overall had enjoyed the experience. Would he do it again? Probably, he said. Others were less enthusiastic when pressed. Some threesomes can go horribly wrong. A woman phoned into a radio station and explained how she was with a couple who broke up while she was sandwiched between them, naked.

Love does not adhere to rules, boundaries, geography or age. A 48-year-old lawyer from Estonia was with a 104-year-old girlfriend, who was the widow of the man's grandfather. Even though she lived in a nursing home before her death, they claimed that the age gap was irrelevant. The man said people were more sceptical of an older man with a younger woman than the other way round, but 'love doesn't ask the age'.

A Bumble survey of about 25,000 daters worldwide who use the app found that they were widening their age filters and were more open to people much older or younger. They were also more conscious of social and political causes, and were less worried about settling down and achieving societal milestones.

Some couples choose other arrangements, such as swinging or open relationships, to keep the spark alive. There is some evidence that swingers have a lower divorce rate than their monogamous peers; this, however, might not be to do with the swinging but with the couple's emotional alignment in the first place. Unconventionality can take other forms. Helena Bonham Carter and Tim Burton decided to live in separate houses, perhaps to avoid inevitable arguments over the state of the bathroom.

Societal norms and expectations matter not a jot. What's important is that everyone – whether that's two, three or more – is happy with the arrangement.

What do the Stoics say?

Ancient Romans had a heightened sense of individualism that was not far removed from our own self-obsessed times, according to Charlotte Higgins, author of Latin Love Lessons. *She says people of our times connect with the Ancient Roman in our openness about sex. Rome experienced huge sexual changes as the empire expanded. Citizens of the Republic were proud of their prudery, but the political revolution that gave rise to the imperial era coincided with an age of revolutionary love liaisons – the most scandalous being that between Mark Antony and the Egyptian queen Cleopatra. 'The new culture of pleasure and sophistication brought with it the idea of falling in love as a lifestyle choice,' Higgins wrote.*

The Stoics agreed with the concept of love, but exercised temperance in all their activities, including in the bedroom. They did not allow emotions to control their actions, so one imagines that they did not begin their day with a lust-fuelled orgy. However, they explicitly rejected following convention. 'You should not copy the bad simply because they are many, nor should you hate the many because they are unlike you,' Seneca wrote. Follow a virtuous path, irrespective of whether that aligns with current conventions.

That said, before you start your orgy, bear in mind these words of Marcus Aurelius: 'Never regard something as doing you good if it makes you betray a trust or lose your sense of shame or makes you show hatred, suspicion, ill-will or hypocrisy, or a desire for things best done behind closed doors.'

A FINAL WORD FROM THE STOICS
'First tell yourself what kind of person you want to be, then do what you have to do.'
Epictetus, *Discourses*

RULE 10 Don't worry about rules

RULE 11
Remember, it's not you, it's them (actually, it's probably you)

> 'And the best and the worst of this is
> That neither is most to blame,
> If you have forgotten my kisses
> And I have forgotten your name.'
> Algernon Charles Swinburne, 'An Interlude'

IT IS MUCH easier to blame other people when a date goes badly or a relationship fails. I started seeing Darren, a man who in his spare time liked to produce sci-fi films featuring clay aliens. Certain things troubled me. He paid me no attention when I visited, and instead tinkered with his car or chatted to mates on the phone. On the one occasion I introduced him to my mother, he sniffed her arm and told her she smelled of fly spray, rather than the Chanel No. 5 she was wearing. Later, over a meal, Darren casually mentioned that he had slept with a friend the week before whose house had an ugly white picket fence. Then he said he felt bad being rude about her fence. Naturally, I told him he was the Antichrist and left. After a while, I realised I could not blame him. We were totally misaligned and he simply was not the person for me. I also realise now that he looked like a groundhog.

If there is one thing I have learned in love and in life, it is not to overdo anything. This has been a painful lesson for someone whose self-control is barely visible with chocolate, television, champagne, gossiping, and disliking people with bad personalities – why can't they move to Mars and let the rest of us be? My resolution now is to do everything gently, whether it is concealing my disdain for a detractor at work, dealing with dingbats on the road or delicately smoothing over romantic setbacks.

This approach is the perfect mindset for dating. It is too easy to write someone off after you discover they wear a cape with sandals, have nativity wallpaper in their bedroom or a bedazzled manicure with fake jewels stuck on their nails. Before leaping to judgement, we could let their eccentricities percolate in our minds for a while, and be gently curious before dismissing them as a prospect.

Having said that, there are things to avoid saying on a first date unless you want to kybosh the evening:

- 'Do you want kids?'
- 'Have I told you about my insane ex?'
- 'Do you love me?'
- 'How much do you earn?'
- 'I think monogamy might be outdated ...'
- 'I'm not looking for anything serious now ...'
- 'You must have lots of people after you ...'
- 'I only like people with upturned mouths and ginger hair ...'

Other mates reported difficult encounters that they squarely blamed on their dates.

One friend had a cocktail with a man called Ian, who turned up with rollers in his hair and two horns. 'At the end of the night, he said he was not attracted to me,' my friend said. Another dated a woman called Quoll, who wore a gold and green kaftan and ended up stalking her.

I assured both those friends that the problem was not them. But really it was, because they had specific requirements that did not include rollers, horns or kaftans. The chasm between their expectations and the reality of the encounters was what ended things on a bum note.

What do the Stoics say?

A central tenet of Stoic philosophy is the need to take responsibility for our own choices and actions. In this sense, the issue will always be that you have no direct control over the actions, thoughts and feelings of others. You only have ownership of what you do. If a date goes badly, reflect on the part you played, as this is the only thing you can influence. If you view dating as a screening process, then you might not feel so bad that you wasted an hour on a coffee with a person who blabs on about royal tennis and bulldozes anything you say. Marcus Aurelius urged us to focus on finding strength through exerting control over our mind and not to fruitlessly dwell on outside events.

Darren and I were hopelessly ill-suited, but he was happy with the arrangement. I had to summon courage, face rejection and look for someone much better suited to me. Fearing a future alone with six cats that end up eating your decaying body can drive you towards dating desperation. The future is unknowable, though, so ruminating on a possible life of loneliness is pointless. As Seneca said: 'We suffer more often in imagination than in reality.' However, avoiding dates is also unadvisable. 'While we wait for life, life passes,' Seneca said.

A FINAL WORD FROM THE STOICS

'It is a ridiculous thing for a man not to fly from his own badness, which is indeed possible, but to fly from other men's badness, which is impossible.'
Marcus Aurelius, *Meditations*

RULE 11 Remember, it's not you, it's them

RULE 12
Write a love letter to yourself

**'You, yourself, as much as anybody in the
entire universe, deserve your love and affection.'**
—Buddha

THE BESTSELLING BOOK *8 Rules of Love*, by Jay Shetty, advises that we
must prepare ourselves for love and establish a dialogue with ourselves.
One way to gain more self-awareness is to write a love letter to
yourself. Shetty's example thanks the self for being a loyal companion
throughout the ups and downs of life, noting that the self is the only
person who knows our deepest inner thoughts.

In essence, our self never leaves us and is one of the most reliable
partners we will ever have. Though the self might lead us astray on
occasion, hopefully there is a desire to learn from mishaps. In fact,
our own self embodies unconditional love, according to Shetty's
letter.

Following his lead, I decided to write myself a letter to allow me to
really get to know myself:

Dear self,

Firstly, could you please stop eating chocolate? It's really annoying, as
it is limiting my options for things to wear on a date. Also, could you please
have more self-respect and not go out with people who mistake Chanel for

fly spray, or who say 'and that' after every sentence, or who stare at you blankly after you tell a joke?

You have absolutely no control over when the love of your life will walk into your life – but, equally, be alert so that you grab onto him when he does become available. Don't worry that you got rejected by Ben Keipert in kiss-chasey at primary school. You took a while to blossom, and besides, that kind of rejection makes your personality, because you could not rely on your looks back then.

Also, people find it annoying the way you interrupt them, and you could be a bit tidier. Other than that, you seem nice (some of the time).

Cheerio,

Me

P.S. Don't worry about your webbed chin, as your dates won't notice it if you're sitting front on.

Of course, if the letter fails to spice things up when there is no one on the horizon, you could always marry yourself. There's a meme on social media that says 'I want a small, tasteful wedding. No family. No friends. No groom. Just me eating cake.'

I seriously considered doing this in my mid-30s, mainly because I was sick of buying presents for friends' weddings. Why should I be discriminated against just because I couldn't find anyone who I clicked with enough to walk down the aisle? I didn't marry myself in the end – I married someone else. And the presents were a lovely bonus.

What do the Stoics say?

Stoicism strongly focuses on the self, but does not encourage selfishness. However, the ability to live in solitude is prized. Solitude does not equate to loneliness: you can feel more alone in a crowded room or married to the wrong person than living by yourself at the height of a lockdown. If you're at peace with yourself, solitude can be embraced. We shouldn't be reliant on another person to feel content within ourselves.

RULE 12 Write a love letter to yourself

Contentment from within is a good springboard for finding love elsewhere. 'The wise man should rely on nothing outside himself: he should value only internal goods, that is, virtue and the state of his soul,' author Ruth Caston said. 'It follows that the wise man will be completely free of all passion.' Caston recognised the value of focusing on our inner soul.

Stoicism encourages us to work on ourselves so that we are comfortable in our own company. We are also responsible for our actions. If you're solo and unhappy about that, it is on you to do something about it — no one else can direct your actions. Maybe that means finally signing up to Tinder or Hinge. If everyone is swiping left, then only you have the ability to examine why that is and to do something about it.

A FINAL WORD FROM THE STOICS

'Avoid the many, avoid the few, avoid even the individual. I know of no one with whom I should be willing to have you shared.'
Seneca, 'On Living to Oneself'

RULE 13
Find the right person

**'Marriage is miserable unless you find the right person
that is your soulmate, and that takes a lot of looking.'**
Attributed to Marvin Gaye

WHEN YOU SENSE a subtle shift in mood in your beloved, like an animal detects shifts in barometric pressure or the Earth's magnetic field, then you may just have stumbled across the right person. Someone you can say everything or nothing to, leaving conversational chemtrails like ants to activate your partner's antennae. Home is a person, not a place. And finding the right person is like coming home.

But advising people just to 'find the right person' is a bit like telling someone to win Lotto. If it were so easy, there would be no dating apps, songs would not be dominated by lyrics about love, and rom-coms would not exist.

There are many paths to finding the right person, as we have explored. Susan was advised by her mother to bury a garden gnome upside down in order to find a husband. Absurd though this piece of wisdom sounded, it worked, because the week that the gnome met its early demise, she met the man she would later marry.

Some friends posted on social media about how their partner was the rock they orbited around and the wind beneath their wings. Despite these vomitous declarations, what made their partner right?

They said they took an 'us versus the world' approach to life, they shared their inner struggles, they had lots of fun and they actually did things together (like creating vomit-inducing social media posts).

In reality, we are lucky to find one great love. That's because love does not care about timing, age, geography, socioeconomic status or any other type of boundary. Some people believe instant chemistry happens when you encounter a soulmate. Former NASA roboticist Randall Munroe calculated that most people have a pool of about half a billion people to choose from, if you don't restrict for gender, sexual orientation, culture and language differences. He estimated that the chance of us finding true love is about one in 10,000. Those are grim odds.

If finding the right person were easy, then we'd all live happily ever after. Unfortunately, it is not so straightforward. Just ask Charles and Di, Hugh Jackman and Deborra-Lee Furness, or Leonardo Di Caprio and his plethora of partners. Maybe they were the right person at a given time, but in the end they were incompatible and busted up. No matter how intertwined your lives might be, you are not a single entity. Some couples call themselves 'a unit', 'one team' and even 'one soul split in Atlantan times'. Other couples use the pronoun 'we' for everything. 'We love Thai food but we also like Chinese food for a change.'

According to *Psychology Today Australia*, good relationships are built on several non-negotiable pillars. These include trust, commitment, respect and communication. That means not editing your personality or reactions in case you offend your partner. It means being comfortable to respectfully say what you think without fear of being judged, criticised or shamed. Sharing values, goals and a vision for the future is important for healthy partnerships. And having the freedom to be yourself and change in tandem with your partner. Along with these, I would stress the importance of having fun as a counterweight to the seriousness of adulthood.

Ultimately, the right person should not be hard work and your respective growth paths not wildly out of sync. There is an effortlessness in being with someone you are highly compatible with that does not require strategies, guidance or tactics to keep it on track.

What do the Stoics say?

Mark Antony clearly felt Cleopatra was the right person, so much so that he vowed to kill himself after he heard she had died. He ordered his slave, Eros, to bump him off, but Eros chose to kill himself first, forcing Antony to do the deed himself. Just before he died, he learned that Cleopatra was still alive, and he ordered his servants to bring him to her quarters, where he died by her side. It was a debacle.

Fannia followed her husband, Helvidius Priscus, into exile during the time of Nero. She was also later exiled for providing materials and support to Senecio, the author of a book on her husband's life. Even though the Senate had passed a decree that the books should be destroyed, she took copies into exile with her. Both she and Mark Antony demonstrated truly admirable devotion to their partner.

When you choose your partner, you have to accept them as they are. Life is change — we all have different seasons throughout our lives. The trick is to adapt yourself as your partner and your relationship evolves. Rather than seeking something new, Stoicism teaches us to appreciate what we already have. Author David Fideler, in his book Breakfast with Seneca, *writes: 'Don't dream of what you don't already possess. Instead, think about the great blessings you do have, for which you feel grateful, and remind yourself of how much they'd be missed if they weren't already yours.'*

A FINAL WORD FROM THE STOICS

'Hasten, therefore, in order that, while perfecting yourself for my benefit, you may not have learned perfection for the benefit of another.'
Seneca, 'On the Friendship of Kindred Minds'

RULE 13 Find the right person

RULE 14
Avoid the wrong person

**'I was married by a judge.
I should have asked for a jury.'**
Attributed to Groucho Marx

'I HATE AND LOVE. Why do I do this, perhaps you ask? I don't know. But I feel it's being done to me, and the pain is crucifixion.' This Ancient Roman poem by Catullus captures the feelings of loving the wrong person. You both love and hate them, but you cannot leave them.

Chad believes that trust, respect and chemistry are the foundations of a great relationship. With this mindset, he went on holiday in Denmark and met a local man he assumed was lovely. But there were red flags along the way. First, his date wanted to stop off to buy some magic mushrooms from a drug dealer. As you do. His date then slipped into a David Beckham jersey once they were in his apartment. A shrine to David Beckham stood in his living room, with wall-to-wall posters of the football legend, a pink cushion emblazoned with Beckham's face and a mug that said: 'Today I don't feel like doing anything except David Beckham – I'd do him.' As the mushrooms took effect, Chad's date casually revealed that he had disposed of his last few boyfriends. Chad asked, somewhat nervously, if these boyfriends were okay now. His date shook his head. Cue a rapid exit.

Chad's romantic track record had not been great. In his final years of university, before he was dating men, he had a dalliance with a married white witch called Susanne, whose home he shared as a boarder. Chad believed she used her dark magic to woo him after he had told her he preferred men. He ended up writing her a series of love letters, which her husband found. Chad was swiftly kicked out of the house. Just before his final exams, the white witch told Chad she was pregnant with his baby, which turned out to be fake.

Perhaps because of his patchy dating history, Chad now has the ability to identify the wrong people and avoid similar scenarios in the future. He says spark, physical chemistry and humour make a date relationship-worthy, but maintaining this in the long run is difficult. Finding chemistry with someone is difficult enough. But finding someone compatible who has not bumped off their previous partners is a good start.

For Mark, the clues were no less unsubtle. He got together with a former work colleague, Roxanne, who was on the rebound from a long-distance relationship that had finally succumbed to the realities of geography. They got on fine at first but it quickly slipped into a moribund relationship that became increasingly unbalanced. They were drinking a bottle of wine every night to get in the mood, because sex had become a chore. One day, as Mark changed out of his work clothes, he saw in the wardrobe a meringue-like wedding dress complete with veil, tiara and five-metre wedding train. That was his cue to call a hard stop to the relationship.

In response to Mark ending things, Roxanne sewed prawns into the hems of the curtain in the living room, left a rotting trout behind the washing machine, stole his passport and put dishwasher salt in the kettle.

One thing to avoid is keeping someone warm on the sidelines. It might be an ex or a past date you have on the backburner just in case things go pear-shaped with your current love interest. Apart from simply being mean, it might prevent your backup from developing their own relationships into something more significant.

What do the Stoics say?

Sometimes our heart — or other organs — rule our head and we end up with someone we shouldn't. We haven't exercised self-control and wisdom in our decisions. And do you know why we don't have the power to attain this Stoic ideal? It is because we are in love with our vices, and we make excuses for them instead of shaking them off. Seneca said: 'We mortals have been endowed with sufficient strength by nature, if only we use this strength, if only we concentrate our powers and rouse them all to help us or at least not to hinder us. The reason is unwillingness, the excuse, inability.'

If love teaches us anything, it is the futility of pushing on with someone who does not nourish our soul, in contravention of the Stoic virtues of wisdom and courage. Seneca reminds us repeatedly that time is a finite resource, and spending it with the wrong person is wasting both our time and theirs. 'It is not that we have a short space of time, but that we waste much of it,' he said. Even if you have spent a lot of time with the wrong person, the Stoic approach is to put it behind you: all of our living takes place in the present.

A FINAL WORD FROM THE STOICS

'Even the storm, before it gathers, gives a warning; houses crack before they crash; and smoke is the forerunner of fire. But damage from man is instantaneous, and the nearer it comes the more carefully it is concealed.'
Seneca, 'On the Dangers of Association with Our Fellow-Men'

RULE 14 Avoid the wrong person

RULE 15
Don't ignore personality

**'The meeting of two personalities is like the
contact of two chemical substances:
if there is any reaction, both are transformed.'**

Carl Jung, *Modern Man in Search of a Soul*

IN OUR LOOKS-BASED society, the quality of a dating app profile photo
largely determines the direction of swipes and how many hits you get.
Which explains why most people put up a picture that either is ten
years old or heavily photoshopped, or features heavy machinery that
obscures their face. A few quirky, endearing and possibly fabricated
facts about personality offer almost no insight into a person's character.
Messaging with a prospective date is about as useful at filling in the
personality gaps as when we tell the interviewer at a job interview that
our biggest flaw is working too hard.

Attraction is the fuel that triggers the chemical spark of romance,
but a relationship based on looks alone is bound to struggle if one
person is utterly humourless and the other is addicted to fun. Of
course, the looks-to-personality ratio differs for everyone.

When asked for his desired looks-to-personality ratio, my mate
Tim said 40:60. 'You need the 40 per cent for sexual attraction,'
he said. 'You're not going to sleep in the same bed for decades with
someone who looks like a rotting carcass.' But looks fade and long

partnerships involve long conversations over many decades, and that's why Tim felt personality was the more important factor.

Others have far more superficial entry-level criteria. This is different for everyone, of course. But Tim's logic is sound: the reality is that personality will have a bigger influence on the success of the relationship than looks. If it was given equal footing to looks in the first place, that might save a few failed relationships.

It certainly seems true that our physical attractiveness may shape our personality and behaviour. At 14, I was in Year 9 at an all-girls school, and attended a mandatory dancing class with boys from an all-boys school. We lined up on one side in a church hall and waited for boys to ask us to dance. For context, I wore a peppermint skirt, had a Joan Jett haircut and silver braces that covered the entire surface area of my teeth. Unsurprisingly, no one asked me to dance and I was left like a shag on a rock while I watched my friends dance with boys for the first time. The attractive girls formed coalitions with other attractive girls, and as a collective exuded magnetism and confidence. But it cleared a path for me to develop a vast network of friends, and a love of space and writing. I eventually entered the world of dating when my grooming improved, armed with a big dollop of curiosity and a repertoire of stories about my teenage mishaps for any would-be romantic partner.

Dr Christian Jarrett, editor of the British Psychological Society's Research Digest blog, outlined a theory that suggests our personalities develop in line with our genetic traits, such as size, strength and attractiveness. This even impacts our ability to find romantic partners and our political beliefs. And it may explain why some physically imposing people tend to also be extroverts. A University of Göttingen study of 200 men in Germany found that men with larger chests, biceps and greater physical strength tended to be more assertive and physically active.

This merely reinforced that personality is vital for longevity in relationships after the initial rush of lust hormones slows to a trickle and the focus shifts to being able to amuse one another for the next 50 years.

What do the Stoics say?

The Stoics found beauty in the natural world, in human nature and in our universal nature. Physical appearance was not a prerequisite for beauty. That said, discipline in your grooming and presentation was valued, as they contribute to your life purpose and goals.

As with everything, moderation was the key. Seneca warned against 'repellent attire, unkempt hair, slovenly beard, open scorn of silver dishes, a couch on the bare earth, and any other perverted forms of self-display'. An inward philosophical mindset and an exterior that conformed to society was the optimum, but 'do not wear too fine, nor yet too frowzy, a toga'.

Seneca was no fan of body-building. In a letter titled 'On Brawn and Brains', he said it was foolish 'for a cultivated man to work hard over developing the muscles and the broadening the shoulders and strengthening the lungs'. By 'overloading the body with food you strangle the soul and render it less active'. Too much exercise, he felt, wasted our precious 'life-force' and rendered it 'less fit to bear a strain'. He advocated short and simple exercises that 'tire the body rapidly' and 'so save our time', because 'time is something of which we ought to keep strict account'. Running, weights and high jumping were acceptable – 'but whatever you do, come back soon from body to mind', as 'the mind must be exercised both day and night'.

A FINAL WORD FROM THE STOICS

'That which is really beautiful has no need of anything; not more than law, not more than truth, not more than benevolence or modesty.'
Marcus Aurelius, *Meditations*

RULE 15 Don't ignore personality

RULE 16
Find someone to do nothing with

'The best things in life are free
The stars belong to everyone
They gleam there for you and me'

Buddy DeSylva and Lew Brown

A LAZY SATURDAY with your beloved can be bliss when the afternoon stretching before you does not involve chores or family obligations or social engagements. Happily pottering or lazing about in comfortable silence is a sign of closeness. It is much easier to find a shared purpose to distract you from the reality of the relationship. Binge-watching TV thrillers, snorkelling in coral reefs or bird watching are lovely activities. But a true test is whether the relationship flourishes in the *absence* of an activity.

There are mental and physical benefits to doing nothing, even for the briefest time, according to *Psychology Today*. It offers a reprieve from the relentless busyness we associate with a productive life. The prospect of ignoring an overflowing to-do list makes people twitchy if they are accustomed to ticking off items. Doing nothing with your partner provides the space for the intrusion of uncomfortable thoughts for those prone to worrying. In this case, punctuating nothing with something pleasant may help.

Jeremy met Scarlett through a dating site as he was yearning for someone to do things with. They regularly went to the movies, the theatre, the pub, on holidays and even volunteered together. They never stopped. Finally, things got serious and they moved in together. They fell into a routine where they went out separately with friends. That was until Jeremy had a cycling accident and was forced to convalesce at home for two months.

They had never spent long stretches of time doing nothing together before. After a time, their conversation lost its spark. They squabbled over the telly, rarely agreeing on a show they both liked. Scarlett increasingly went out with friends, until one day she never came back.

Some people in long-term relationships reach a level of comfort where they leave the bathroom door open when doing their business, and treat their partner like a pair of well-worn slippers. Did they want to seduce their spouse when they emerged from the shower? No. Did they want to rip off their work clothes when they walked in the door at the end of the day? Absolutely not. But was this someone they could do nothing with? Totally.

Early in a relationship, you send texts to one another that say, 'I can't wait to see you,' and you plan romantic getaways to spend even more time together. Fast-forward a decade: now children may be part of the picture, and work demands have increased in complexity. The relationship becomes more comfortable, predictable, boring even. But it can still be a successful partnership if you are so content with one another that you can do nothing together.

A relationship that requires constant activity is in danger.

What do the Stoics say?

The Stoics believed in living in the moment, as we have no control over either the past or the future. They did believe in taking action, of course, but not simply for the sake of it. Instead, we should value the beauty of the moment, as each is a gift. That might mean just sitting and reading the paper while your partner watches The Real Housewives of Beverly Hills, or crocheting a tea cosy in the shape of a badger while your partner cleans out the cat litter, or just doing nothing at all.

Seneca quoted a Greek proverb that said: 'The fool's life is empty of gratitude and full of fears; its course lies wholly toward the future.' He believed this meant we are 'plunged by our blind desires into ventures which will harm us, but certainly will never satisfy us … nor do we reflect how pleasant it is to demand nothing, how noble it is to be contented and not to be dependent on Fortune.' Why demand something of the future when you can practise not craving for such things?

The present moment is the only reality in time: the past is gone and cannot be changed, and the future is yet to exist. That means only the present can be savoured. Marcus Aurelius advised letting go of the past, trusting in providence for the future and revering the present.

We use diversions to escape reality, to forget briefly the past or the future. In a good relationship, we shouldn't require bungee jumping off a bridge to stay interested. We can appreciate a present moment of nothingness together.

A FINAL WORD FROM THE STOICS
'Be not heavy in business, nor disturbed in conversation, nor rambling in your thoughts … you must always preserve in yourself the virtues of freedom, of sincerity, sobriety, and good nature.'
Marcus Aurelius, *Meditations*

RULE 16 Find someone to do nothing with

PART TWO
RELATIONSHIPS

'When you realise you want to spend the rest of
your life with somebody, you want the rest
of your life to start as soon as possible.'

Billy Crystal in *When Harry Met Sally*

EARLY IN A NEW RELATIONSHIP ...

LISTEN TO: 'I'm into Something Good', The Bird and the Bee; 'The
Honeymoon Song', Everclear; 'I'm Beginning to See the Light', Ella Fitzgerald
DON'T LISTEN TO: 'Dear Future Husband', Meghan Trainor; 'I Still Haven't
Found What I'm Looking For', U2; 'Forever and Ever', Demis Roussos
EAT: Plenty of carbs (to make up for the first few weeks of no eating)
DON'T EAT: Beans (at least too early in the relationship)
DRINK: Water (for hydration) and plenty of cocktails
DON'T DRINK: To excess
WATCH: *When Harry Met Sally*
DON'T WATCH: *The Wedding Singer*; *My Best Friend's Wedding* (too soon)
READ: *Everything I Know about Love* by Dolly Alderton
DON'T READ: *Fifty Shades of Grey* by E.L. James (too soon)

LATER IN THE RELATIONSHIP ...

LISTEN TO: 'We Belong Together', Ritchie Valens; 'Hold on to Me', The Black Sorrows; 'I Stand Corrected', Vampire Weekend

DON'T LISTEN TO: 'Toxic', Britney Spears; 'Everyday I Love You Less and Less', Kaiser Chiefs

EAT: A well-balanced diet, plus plenty of chocolate to keep your spirits up

DON'T EAT: Too much chocolate

DRINK: In moderation – have several alcohol-free days a week

DON'T DRINK: A bottle of wine a night

WATCH: *One Day*; *Broadchurch*; *Game of Thrones*

DON'T WATCH: *The War of the Roses*; *Revolutionary Road*

READ: *The Adventure Challenge, Couples Edition*; *How to Be an Adult in Relationships* by David Richo; *Sex for Lazy People: 50 Effortless Positions So You Can Do It without Overdoing It*, Ginny Hogan

DON'T READ: *Wuthering Heights* by Emily Brontë; *Gone Girl* by Gillian Flynn

Once we have macheted our way through the dating jungle to find our own oasis of love, we must all play the long game to keep the romantic fires burning. Stoic wisdom can help us keep boredom and temptation at bay, navigate blow-ups and disputes, and avoid letting the relationship become a charred rump of resentment. In the first instance, finding the right person will set the partnership up for success. And if you think you can do better, maybe they can too.

A key ingredient to a successful union is to invest both in the relationship and in building your own life and agency. Simply being married or attached is not enough to sustain a meaningful, long-term relationship. Telling your other half they cannot leave the house unless they declutter the medicine cabinet is a sure-fire way to kill a partnership.

As we all know, you can be happy or you can be right. Anyone who thinks you can be both should get used to being single. Pausing before you respond to a verbal jab and adopting an 'us versus the world' approach will stand the relationship in good stead.

RULE 17
Learn the language of love

**'The limits of my language
mean the limits of my world.'**

Ludwig Wittgenstein, *Tractatus Logico-Philosophicus*

UNDERSTANDING YOUR PARTNER'S 'love language' is essential if you're going to keep the fires of romance burning bright.

Love languages, Gary Chapman says in his book *The 5 Love Languages: The Secret to Love That Lasts*, are the ways we receive and express love in a relationship. Based on his observations as a marriage counsellor, they include words of affirmation, quality time, physical touch, acts of service and gifts. Speaking your partner's love language makes them feel loved. Chapman had a eureka moment when his own marriage hit a rough patch, and he discovered that his wife valued help around the house, while he needed affirmation to feel loved.

My love language entails coffee in bed, a well-stocked cupboard of chocolate and plenty of compliments, even if in the morning I look like a mummified racoon. But it does not end there. I have discovered I require more from a partner: poems about planets, stars, clouds and love; a mutual love of sci-fi books and films (specifically the film *Interstellar*); and someone to stargaze with and speculate on the existence of aliens. If they also share my enthusiasm for Duran Duran, Supergrass and Regurgitor, so much the better.

My love language also excludes heated arguments in favour of frank and constructive feedback, and prioritises tranquil, sensitive, funny and thoughtful communications. It also requires a partner who is willing to endure my habit of repeating myself, overreacting and interrupting (which is, admittedly, annoying). And one who is into micro displays of affection such as a hand squeeze, a peck on the cheek or a brief back rub. Naturally, all this has shrunk my pool of possible love matches to 0.00001 per cent of humans.

Decoding the love language of men has been much more straightforward: basically it's sex. And maybe a coffee in bed.

Words and encouragement, compliments, uplifting quotes, love letters and loving text messages are good examples of ways to speak your partner's love language. For others, getting off the phone and giving them your undivided attention is what they need to feel loved – maybe even a date or a romantic weekend away. Physical affection is the primary love language for many people, not just through sex but by holding hands, hugging, kissing and touching. For others, their love language involves showing care and concern through doing household chores or errands. As with any new language, mastery takes time, patience and effort.

Paying close attention to your partner's non-verbal cues can tell you when things are less peachy. Think short, clipped answers to questions, a lack of eye contact, no physical touch and no declarations of love. Silence can be a sign of comfort and security, but if it feels strained then there is probably an issue you need to address.

What do the Stoics say?

Epictetus reminds us that happiness can only be found within. Even so, the Stoics valued good communication and appreciating others' perspectives. As we have seen, they saw love and affection as the basis of society. As Seneca put it, 'Society can only remain healthy through the mutual protection and love of its parts.' That's a principle we can apply to all facets of our relationship, including to the unique love language each couple develops.

Seneca believed that love, affection and gratitude were the three critical ingredients. The last of these takes many forms – sacred, cosmic, secular and personal – and is a foundation for all relationships, romantic, professional and societal. Remember to express your gratitude for all thoughtful gestures, even something as small as coffee in bed.

A FINAL WORD FROM THE STOICS

'There is not a man who, when he has benefited his neighbour, has not benefited himself.'
Seneca, 'On Benefits'

RULE 17 Learn the language of love

RULE 18
Don't love-bomb

**'How do I love thee?
Let me count the ways ...'**
Elizabeth Barrett Browning, *Sonnets from the Portuguese*

IN THE 1980s, I love-bombed tennis player Pat Cash when he was at the height of his career. I wrote a letter on pink paper, which was sprayed with perfume and covered in love heart stickers before sending it to an address I believed to be his parents' house in Melbourne. I proposed we marry, failing to consider the reputational consequences for his career should he take on an underage bride, and also ignoring possible resistance from my parents. My mother was busy love-bombing Rod Stewart, though, so I may have got away with it. Fortunately, Pat ghosted me before the term 'ghosting' became commonplace.

Some of my friends who have been happily partnered up for eons have not even heard of love-bombing. Or ghosting. Or breadcrumbing. For the rest of us who have done a bit more relationship hopping, these are terms we must acquaint ourselves with as we search for love. 'Love-bombing' means making grand displays of affection early in a relationship that are disproportionate to where you are on the relationship continuum. Its purpose is to use all your romantic ammunition to lure another person. To be a love-bomber, you need to think you are in love with someone so badly it hurts, and plan a grand romantic gesture – such as having their name skywritten in a love heart – and be prepared to pay for it. Some love-bombers are narcissists – but not all of us, thank you very much.

We should all be wary, though, because love-bombers can turn nasty down the track once they have reeled in their victim. Relationships that burn brightly can just as quickly go up in flames. Telling someone they are the one after a couple of dates could be an attempt to flatter them into submission. Usually, people wait until they establish trust before they say they want to be together forever in this and subsequent lifetimes.

Sometimes, love-bombing goes dramatically wrong. Like in *Miranda*, when the titular character tries to woo her crush, Gary, with a romantic picnic before a flock of geese trample on the food. *Love Actually* features a character called Mark who hires a full band in the chapel where his best friend is marrying, and later serenades his best mate's wife with Christmas carols, which is a bit out of order. In *Raiders of the Lost Ark*, a student of Indiana Jones blinks at him and has 'love you' written on her eyelids during his lecture, leaving him flustered.

Grand gestures are innocent unless they are used to assert control over vulnerable people or to get something in return. An ABC article reports that love-bombing was coined by cult leaders of the Unification Church of the United States to recruit new members by lavishing them with praise and affection. Apparently, it has been practised for centuries by kings and suitors seeking partners. If gestures are frequent and orchestrated in front of others to show off, then you may decide to treat this as a red flag.

What do the Stoics say?
Marcus Aurelius understood that it is normal for us to desire things that are not good for us, but he did not see gifts as objects of desire, viewing them as transient and therefore unimportant. In Meditations *he described a technique for looking at the reality of what you desire:*

'Where things appear most plausible, be sure to bring them to the test, and look at their worthlessness, and strip them of all the words by which they were exalted. Without this care, figure and appearance are great cheats; and when you think your fancy is best employed, you will be most fooled.'

When someone tries to lure you with a grand gesture, it is worth examining what appeals. Are you attracted by the status or power attached to it? Or by the feeling of being desired? Or by the look or feel of the gift itself?

The Stoics believed our progress was thwarted by future emotions, including desire and fear, and present ones such as pleasure and distress. Marcus believed the source of our desire was our principles and actions, which are within our control and can be guided by the critical virtues of temperance and justice. A love bomb is not necessarily unvirtuous, but it can be when it adversely impacts others.

A FINAL WORD FROM THE STOICS

'When you imagine some pleasure, beware that it does not carry you away, like other imaginations. Wait a while, give yourself pause. Next remember two things: how long will you enjoy the pleasure and next how long will you afterwards repent and revile yourself. And set on the other side the joy and self-satisfaction you will feel if you refrain.'

Epictetus, *Enchiridion*

RULE 19
Minimise fibs

'Knowledge is of two kinds.
We know a subject ourselves, or we know
where we can find information upon it.'

Samuel Johnson, quoted in *Life of Samuel Johnson*, James Boswell

WHEN YOUR PARTNER is taking you out for dinner and asks you how long you'll take to get ready and you say, 'Five minutes,' you know this is an outright fib, as you still need to jump into the shower and wash and dry your hair, plus you have no idea what you'll wear.

Sometimes a seemingly insignificant fib can backfire. Underestimating the number of your previous sexual partners might rebound on you if they discover that eight really means 80. Or if you're asked about a new handbag and insist it is eons old, and then the recent receipt turns up when your partner is cleaning the car.

Let's face it, little lies in a relationship are standard. But, as a collective, a steady stream of fibs might erode trust over time. One way to iron out any wrinkles in a relationship is greater transparency over new purchases, or more accurate time assessment when you're getting ready.

To determine compatibility and set up a relationship for future success, it may even be useful to get some insights into love, family, downtime and who will empty the lint from the dryer. Questions might be something along the lines of:

1. What do you do to unwind?
2. Are you into PDA?
3. What makes you feel loved?
4. How will we manage money?
5. Who will empty the food that collects in the kitchen sink plug?
6. What are our boundaries with privacy?
7. How will we manage disagreements?
8. How much time will we spend with extended family?
9. What things annoy you about me?
10. How will we maintain our independence?
11. What are our deal breakers?
12. What are our future goals?

Showing gratitude and appreciation for small things, being affectionate and setting boundaries will put the relationship on the pathway to success. Finding ways to manage the whirling chaos of external events that don't inflict damage on the relationship is vital. Think bubble baths, binge-watching TV froth, cooking for those who find it relaxing, or taking care of pets. Establishing a transparent approach to finances, a fair division of household chores and a shared outlook for the future is always useful before cohabiting.

After the hormonal high we experience early in a relationship subsides, we embark on the next stage: living together. What could be better than being with your beloved 24/7? The image we projected before shacking up may have been based on some minor lies about our cleanliness and hygiene standards and disdain for people who think households 'should be run'. After a few months, though, you realise the love of your life is rattled by the tumbleweeds of lint balls rolling down the hallway, flies buzzing around the rotten fruit bowl or dirty bed sheets that could walk themselves off the bed and into the washing machine. There is nothing like sharing a space with another adult to bring the honeymoon phase to a crashing halt.

RULE 19 Minimise fibs

Before taking the plunge, compare your routines honestly. Are they a night owl or an early riser? Do they mind friends dropping in? What are they like with cleanliness? Disclosing your expectations – and developing some shared ground rules – is a good start.

What do the Stoics say?

Lying was not in the Stoic wheelhouse: deceptiveness and dishonesty were considered the opposite of Stoic virtues. According to the Epitome of Stoic Ethics *by the 1st century BCE author Arius Didymus, Stoics agreed that there were exceptions to this rule: we can 'sometimes employ falsehood in several ways without assenting [to it]; for [he will do so] when a general against his adversaries and in the provision of what is advantageous and in many other aspects of managing life'.*

The Stoics also advocated setting boundaries and establishing limits that reflected their principles of virtue, wisdom and self-discipline. Boundaries require consideration of the feelings of others involved, but are challenging for people pleasers, who deplete their own reserves of patience and goodwill in order to keep everyone else happy.

As for 'love language': the Stoics did not have hearts of stone. They regarded love and affection as primary human emotions. Seneca believed the Stoics had more love for humanity than any other philosophical school, and that this was the bedrock of society. Seneca wrote prolifically about love, affection and gratitude, and his writings indicate a deep understanding of the different kinds of love.

A FINAL WORD FROM THE STOICS

'You have seen those things, look now at these: do not trouble yourself, make yourself simple. Does a man do wrong? He does wrong to himself.'
Marcus Aurelius, *Meditations*

RULE 20
Don't ask your partner what they're thinking

> 'The important thing is not to
> think much but to love much.'
>
> St Teresa of Ávila

AN ONLINE JOKE contrasts the diaries of a woman with those of her spouse. In an expansive entry, the woman laments that her husband has been 'acting weird'. They met at a bar in the evening after she'd been shopping with friends, and the 'conversation wasn't flowing' so she suggested they go somewhere quiet to talk. When he didn't say much, she asked him what was wrong. 'Nothing,' he said. Was it her fault he was upset, she asked. He reassured her it was nothing to do with her and not to worry. During the drive home, she told him she loved him and he 'smiled slightly, and kept driving'. 'I can't explain his behaviour,' the woman wrote. 'I don't know why he didn't say, "I love you, too."'

Back at home she feared she 'had lost him completely, as if he wanted nothing to do with me any more'. After a period of silence in which he seemed 'distant and absent' as he watched TV, she went to bed. Fifteen minutes later, he joined her in bed, and 'to my surprise, he responded to my caress, and we made love', she recorded.

Even so, he seemed 'distracted, and his thoughts were somewhere else'. When he fell asleep, she cried and despaired that perhaps 'his thoughts are with someone else'. 'My life is a disaster,' she concluded.

Her husband's diary entry was more succinct. It simply said: 'My footy team lost, but at least I got a shag.'

The joke speaks to the difficulty of mind reading, as we can never really know what other people are thinking. Although there are times we can probably guess, as this meme suggests: 'Me calling my husband to get me something sweet on the way home but adding "don't worry if you can't" when he actually should worry if he can't.'

How many times have we asked the dreaded question: 'What are you thinking?' It is an utterly pointless, open-ended question. The trouble with contrasting communication styles is that it leaves one person to fill in the silence with their own catastrophic narrative. If a partner is silent, then it must mean something is wrong. Best to be specific if we want to get inside our partner's mind. 'That meal was a bit cheesy, don't you think?' 'How about that bloke's piercing laugh in the restaurant? It was pretty grating, don't you think?' 'Isn't it annoying having to participate in the global economy and work *all the time*?' Or maybe just don't hook up with a quiet person if you like a lot of conversation.

For those of us who have the tendency to fill conversational gaps with a steady cadence of unfiltered commentary, full disclosure of the swirling thoughts occupying our brain can be overwhelming for silent types. Stemming the flow of verbal diarrhoea is well within our power. But asking direct questions might get the response we need to satisfy our curiosity. Conversely, dishing out the silent treatment is not advisable for the above reasons.

Most people are consumed with their own thoughts anyway. Some of us spend hours speculating with our friends over wine and chips what our partners could possibly be thinking. Maybe it really is just about the footy.

What do the Stoics say?

If your partner barely speaks to you, causing you to conjure up frantic thoughts about how the relationship is on life support, consider that they could just be an introvert. As we have explored, Stoicism encourages greater ownership of our thoughts, our actions and our responses to situations. That does not give us licence to overthink situations, and becoming aware of rumination is enough to reduce the overthinking cycle. Our thoughts are neither truthful, solid nor permanent. The Stoics closely monitored their thoughts and feelings, separating their judgements and opinions from attention and wisdom.

Overthinking is fuelled by anxiety and prevents us from living in the present and focusing on what we can control. We cannot control our partner's thoughts, so ruminating over them is pointless.

A FINAL WORD FROM THE STOICS

'One's own mind is a place most free from the crowd and noise in the world, if a man's thoughts are such as to ensure him perfect tranquillity within, and this tranquillity consists in the good ordering of the mind.'

Marcus Aurelius, *Meditations*

RULE 20 Don't ask your partner what they're thinking

RULE 21
Don't get married

**'Marriage is a wonderful invention,
but then again, so is a bicycle repair kit.'**
Attributed to Billy Connolly

A FEW YEARS AGO, on a girls' trip to Las Vegas, my friends and I were
in a limousine, drinking margaritas and listening to 'Toxic' by Britney
Spears at top volume. Maybe it was the alcohol, maybe it was Britney, or
maybe it was the state of our relationships. But we all squeezed through
the sunroof and screamed out 'DON'T DO IT!' to a couple walking, not
driving, up to a drive-through wedding chapel. We weren't opposed
to marriage altogether. But it's long been clear that, in heterosexual
unions, marriage benefits the man more than the woman.

The joke that 'to some, marriage is a word; to others it is a
sentence' is a familiar trope for unhappily married couples. Some
people marry for the prestige in their community of being in a long
marriage, regardless of the relationship quality. Maybe the domestic
and financial loads are unevenly spread. A new term has emerged for
married women who carry the domestic load: 'married single mums'.
These are prevalent in households where there is not an egalitarian
division of labour and investment in career. After Covid-19 forced one
woman to isolate from her husband for a week, she shared a picture
of the kitchen in their home when she eventually emerged. She was

stunned to discover a towering pile of dirty dishes spilling out from the sink and onto the kitchen bench, and the stench of rotting food. For those in more egalitarian relationships, dividing and conquering chores is the only way to keep a household and a marriage afloat.

If people are down on marriage, why does it remain a life goal for so many of us? Australian author Clementine Ford, in her book *I Don't: The Case Against Marriage*, argues that marriage is a patriarchal construct designed to oppress women. She rails against the reality that women in heterosexual marriages carry the domestic and parenting load. Married women with children often submit to taking an economic back seat, which leaves them disadvantaged financially and socially.

But the outlook for men within marriage can be every bit as bleak depending on the relationship dynamic and power balance.

People say marriage means the death of intimacy, but so does permanent singlehood. You don't have to be single to feel lonely and starved of intimacy, but feeling alone and unloved in a marriage could be worse.

People marry for all sorts of reasons. Some like the status of being someone's husband or wife. Others marry because they believe this solidifies their relationship and is a public affirmation of their love and commitment. I once met someone who viewed their wedding simply as an opportunity to stock up on toasters, vases and satin sheets. That union, unsurprisingly, did not last long.

A family friend, Alison, had her ornate dress, garden venue, lavish catering and 150 guests all booked for her wedding. She had turned 40 and the wedding was a long-held dream for her. A week before the big day, though, her husband-to-be pulled the pin with no explanation. She was devastated, but held a party anyway on the day that would have been her wedding. We had champagne and canapes, and toasted the jilted bride, who sat miserably wearing her bridal veil. It was about as fun as a funeral.

What do the Stoics say?

The Stoics believed we can develop excellent moral character regardless of our circumstances — whether we're rich or poor, in good or ill health, married or not married. They supported radical egalitarianism: while it is better if you have natural advantages, it's possible to develop a virtuous character regardless of your circumstances. Some might view the lack of a marriage as a misfortune, while others see the many benefits of staying single: you have more control over your life when it is not complicated by squabbles over money, chores and sex.

Not marrying is either a decision made consciously or a reality foisted upon you. Either way, there is freedom in being the master of your fate and the captain of your soul. The first line of Seneca's famous letters reveals much about his focus on spiritual independence: 'Continue, dear Lucilius, to free yourself: gather and protect your time, which until now has been taken from you, stolen from, or simply vanquished.'

Some regard marriage as a social prison. The Stoics understood the impermanence and transience of life and love, and accepted that even if you do marry, it might not last. That's probably a good thing to keep in mind when the laundry needs folding on a Sunday morning and you would rather be drinking chocolate milk in your underpants while watching Selling Sunset.

A FINAL WORD FROM THE STOICS

'You ... should remind yourself that what you love is mortal, that what you love is not your own. It is granted to you for the present while, and not irrevocably, nor for ever, but like a fig or a bunch of grapes in the appointed season; and if you long for it in the winter, you are a fool.'
Epictetus, *Discourses*

RULE 21 Don't get married

RULE 22
Get married

'I love being married.
It's so great to find one special person
you want to annoy for the rest of your life.'
Attributed to Rita Rudner

IN MAY 1955, *Housekeeping Monthly* published 'The Good Wife's Guide', which encouraged housewives to have dinner ready for their husbands, to 'be a little gay and a little more interesting for him', and to 'prepare the children' in an effort to minimise noise when he comes home. The guide encouraged ladies to 'be happy to see him', 'let him talk first' and never to complain, in order to create peace and tranquillity. Finally, arrange his pillows, take off his shoes and do not under any circumstances ask him any questions, because 'he is the master of the house'. In other words, be a miserable doormat.

But marriage need not be so repressive. If our Aussie Queen Mary of Denmark has taught us anything, it is that getting married can transform your life. At least she does not need to arrange her husband's pillows or take off his shoes. Or cook, or fold the laundry. She reportedly met King Frederik in a chance encounter at the Slip Inn pub in Darling Harbour during the Sydney Olympics in 2000. Her transformation from Tasmanian real estate agent to queen is the stuff of fairytales.

As with all fairytales, though, it has not been without controversy. Speculation that her husband may have been distracted in 2023 by a glamourous Mexican socialite prompted a flurry of media pics of 'our Mary' looking frostier than usual in the presence of her spouse. As the Stoics knew, our struggles disappear over time, and change means that you not only lose but gain as well. Mary gained a promotion to Queen of Denmark after her mother-in-law apparently sought to rein in her son by abdicating.

The rest of us non-royals still benefit from marriage. For some it is everything and others nothing, just a piece of paper and a decent celebration. Either way, the commitment brings comfort that there is someone out there who will look after you following a bad day in the office, or bring you paracetamol when you get sick. All going well, you hope you made the right choice. You are attuned to your spouse's shifts in mood, accepting their foibles and applauding their victories as part of an enduring double act.

Interestingly, married couples in a crowd are less likely to bump into other people. Takayuki Kanda at Kyoto University in Japan analysed hundreds of hours of pedestrian footage and determined that the stronger social interactions between romantic couples meant they were less likely to collide with other people than pairs of co-workers or friends.

A Purdue University team in the United States found that married men and married women live an average of two years longer than their unmarried counterparts, thanks to the influence of shared healthy behaviours. Together, married couples eat more healthily and smoke and drink less. Women look out for the health of their male spouses, but men are less inclined to worry about the health of their female spouses (probably because they don't need to as they get a daily report).

Research also connects loneliness and a lack of close relationships with chronic inflammation linked to heart disease, arthritis, cancers and autoimmune diseases – although married women with unsupportive husbands also showed increased rates of inflammation. But it's not all doom and gloom for unmarried people. Maintaining strong social connections, reducing stress and prioritising a healthy lifestyle can put you up there with your married friends.

What do the Stoics say?

The power, position and prestige of marriage have evolved over the centuries. But societal approval is not enough for success in modern marriage. To thrive, those in a marriage must work on it, not just revel in its social status. It's fair to say that values around marriage 2000 years ago were not entirely the same as in the twenty-first century. For instance, this section of a poem by Catullus conveys almost no aura of romance whatsoever:

It is not right to reject the man to whom your father and mother gave you. You must obey them. Your virginity is not entirely yours. One-third of it belongs to your father, one-third to your mother, and only one-third to you yourself. Don't fight against your parents who have surrendered to your husband a dowry and their rights over you.

The Stoics, however, did not write extensively on the subject of marriage. Antipater of Tarsus believed that marriage and families based around the institution served as the cornerstone of the state. Marcus Aurelius and Seneca both wrote lovingly about their wives; Aurelius deified his, Faustina, following her death. Seneca said of his wife: 'Nature produced us related to one another, since she created us from the same source and to the same end ... Let us possess things in common; for birth is ours in common. Our relations with one another are like a stone arch, which would collapse if the stones did not mutually support each other.'

Stoicism is often equated with detachment, but it's wrong to interpret it as opposed to love. The Stoics' detachment can be understood as their recognition of humans' mortality and our inability to control the lives and lifespans of others. For parents such as Marcus Aurelius and Faustina, who lost all but six of their fourteen children before adulthood, such a philosophy would have been important.

A FINAL WORD FROM THE STOICS

'There are three relations: one to your environment, one to the divine cause from which all things come to pass for all, one to those who live at the same time with you.'

Marcus Aurelius, *Meditations*

RULE 23
Have more fun

'There's nothing surer,
The rich get rich and the poor get children.
In the meantime, in between time,
Ain't we got fun.'

Raymond B. Egan and Gus Kahn, 'Ain't We Got Fun'

WHEN YOU MEET someone you think is lovely, it simply never crosses your mind that they might be the sort of human who thinks it's normal to vacuum the house every Friday night instead of going to the pub. Or recount in detail a dream they had the previous night about a disorderly filing cabinet. Before you move in together, you think you have discussed all the areas that can trip up a relationship – finance, kids, pets, religion, parents, property and holidays.

But on the first Friday in your new place, you discover there is one important subject you have overlooked. 'We need to clean the house,' your partner says, as though this is what everyone does at the end of the week. When you explain that you generally like to go to the pub, and that cleaning the house after a tough day is about as appealing as watching a documentary on Hitler, he looks aghast and hands you the vacuum. Tidying 'needed' to be done before fun. The dream ended up being prophetic.

For someone who prioritises fun after a long, hard week, such a union will be short-lived. People who dictate, organise or educate their partner on their way of doing things only damage the relationship. Collaborating, compromising and being true partners in how you live makes both of you feel valued.

The honeymoon phase always wanes as you build a life together, which naturally includes domestic routines such as regular trips to the supermarket, cleaning the toilet and vacuuming the floors. And refraining from yelping when your partner seemingly ignores the brake lights ahead and keeps driving at maximum speed. The visceral excitement of early romance simply cannot be sustained for most couples. Even female dragonflies suffer the same feelings of tedium, faking their own death to get out of mating with their unwanted male partners. At least they do not decapitate their men, like female praying mantises do.

Danish existentialist philosopher Søren Kierkegaard believed we should go deeper into our heart and soul to find the antidote to tedium. His theory was that there are three phases to life. The first is the aesthetic phase, when we seek new experiences, opportunities and delights to cure boredom. The sex, drugs and rock'n'roll phase, if you will. After a while, this becomes trivial and boring. The next ethical phase is going deeper into the unknown, creating a joint existence with another, which can be confronting. Beyond this is the religious phase, where we explore and deepen our faith, whether it be through traditional religion, meditation or whatever spiritual path helps us illuminate and evolve our lives.

Pleasure is fleeting. It can come from eating a Mars Bar or sipping champagne with friends, or going to a holiday resort with your family. These are all external forces that can bring us immense pleasure. According to *The Greatness Guide* by Robin Sharma, happiness and contentment are the DNA of pleasure that comes from within. You can be happy despite facing adversity, because this type of joy is intrinsic, not extrinsic. Riding out the highs and lows of a long marriage or

RULE 23 Have more fun

relationship is much easier when there is a foundation of contentment that can cushion the inevitable setbacks.

We all have a different equilibrium for excitement versus predictability. One person's excitement might be ordering Chinese takeaway on a Tuesday night with their partner. For others, it might mean jumping out of a plane or spicing up their bedroom antics.

Boredom differs from comfort, according to one US article. Comfort is built on trust and the freedom to be yourself with your partner, rather than on an end-to-end adrenaline rush. Relationships stagnate from a lack of investment in shared interests or, conversely, in a lack of individual freedom.

Cognitive reappraisal is a strategy aimed at reprogramming our mindset about the relationship by focusing on a partner's good attributes and how they contribute positively. Take up penguin rescue volunteering, or learn Ethiopian cooking, or buy some glow-in-the-dark sex toys to jump-start the partnership if you feel things have become too comfortable.

What do the Stoics say?

There is an old adage attributed (almost certainly incorrectly) to Plato that says, 'You can discover more about a person in an hour of play than in a year of conversation.' This is why we choose fun places to meet up with a date when we're sizing them up as a potential partner (and, incidentally, why we should conduct job interviews at the pub). While the Stoics themselves were not strictly known as fun-lovers, they enjoyed observing the absurdity of life.

The Stoics weren't against pleasure, but they were against being a slave to desire. So enjoying wine is fine but being an alcoholic isn't. They argued that we should stay in control of our emotions. We shouldn't become obsessive, either in seeking pleasure or in cleaning the house. Neither activity is intrinsically right or wrong.

The Stoics knew that pleasure could be a vice, but equally pleasure could signal a happy state of mind. Pure joy, on the other hand, never ceases because it comes from within. Seneca said that if you 'seek pleasures of all kinds in all directions, you must know that you are as far short of wisdom as you are short of joy'. Joy is our collective path, but pleasures, riches and official titles will merely send us wandering off the path to happiness and towards grief. Joy can be found in an eternally calm mind.

A FINAL WORD FROM THE STOICS

'The wise man is joyful, happy and calm, unshaken; he lives on a plane with the gods ... if day and night your soul keeps on its even and unswerving course, upright and content with itself, then you have attained to the greatest good that mortals can possess.'
Seneca, 'On Pleasure and Joy'

RULE 23 Have more fun

RULE 24
Deal with the big stuff

'Ah, Houston, we've had a problem here.'
Jack Swigert on *Apollo 13*, 14 April 1970

ALL OF US who have been in long-term relationships will know that leaving smears of pasta sauce on the kitchen bench, saying 'aah' after each sip of tea and abandoning toenail clippings on the couch can nibble away at the bank of goodwill. But there is nothing that will diminish relationship capital more than failing to deal with the really big questions, like whether to have kids, how you manage money, whether religion is important, how you manage the work–life balance or infidelity.

There's no doubt that aligning your values at the beginning of a relationship is a good idea. But the trouble is, you need some sort of simulated test to expose your spouse to these situations to really see how they will really react. We almost need a Tamagotchi pet for long-term relationships in order to test a partner in all sorts of domestic settings. How will they react to unsolicited visits from the in-laws? Will they respond with anger, fear, flight or control when things get tough? How will they react to financial setbacks? Or to a different approach to parenting? Will they tackle issues as an individual or can you work as a team when problems come your way? If you can, you may have picked a winner.

Some seemingly small issues are really big issues in disguise. They mask the tectonic cracks in a relationship. For instance, it could be that one of you plays golf all day Saturday and doesn't care whether your kid makes it to football training or chess or jujitsu. How will they be when you need support due to a serious illness or a life crisis? Or maybe your partner never tips in restaurants and is always the last one to the bar to buy a round of drinks at the pub. Will they be willing to spend money on holidays or home improvements?

Tackling the big issues early in a relationship will set it up for greater success, but if the issues emerge later on, then course-correction could prevent derailment. There is no right or wrong way, but finding common ground with your partner and building trust help manage tricky issues.

What do the Stoics say?

The Stoics contemplated the big issues, such as the origins of the universe and what gave rise to life on Earth. They used philosophy as a framework to refine their logic and ability to think and tackle big ideas and significant issues constructively. 'Of all existing things,' said Epictetus, 'some are in our power and others are not in our power.' In the former category are 'thought, impulse, will to get and will to avoid, and, in a word, everything which is our own doing'. Things not in our power include 'the body, property, reputation, office, and, in a word, everything which is not our own doing'.

When managing big and seemingly insurmountable issues that threaten to derail your relationship, it is worth remembering the four cardinal virtues: wisdom, justice, fortitude and temperance. They can equip us with the ability to weather the storms when our relationship hits choppy seas or we're facing other big challenges.

Wisdom gives us the insight to focus only on those things we can control, like choosing a partner, resolving a hiccup in a relationship

*or ditching them if they end up being a bad match. This is perfectly
encapsulated in the famous 'serenity prayer':*

> God, grant me the serenity to accept the things I cannot change,
> the courage to change the things I can,
> and the wisdom to know the difference.

*Our sense of justice empowers us to assess a situation accurately:
whether it is fair, for example, for one parent to ignore a Himalayan
clothing pile that needs folding and instead spend the day at a winery
with friends. Understanding your partner's motivations and state of
mind might mean you conclude that their spending the afternoon with
friends will be better for everyone ... or maybe not.*

*Discussions about delicate issues require pre-planning, timing,
sensitivity — and fortitude. Take the view of a third-party observer.
Would they judge the problem as serious? If the answer is yes, then have
the courage to have the difficult conversation with your beloved rather
than just enduring the status quo. Every day you choose not to tackle
a problem, you are making a decision to put up with it. Temperance,
meanwhile, helps keep a discussion from descending into warfare.*

A FINAL WORD FROM THE STOICS
'The sum of the matter is this: life is short; the
present must be turned to profit with reasonableness
and right. Be sober without effort.'
Marcus Aurelius, *Meditations*

RULE 24 Deal with the big stuff

RULE 25
Don't tell your partner to calm down

**'Wrongs are often forgiven but contempt never is.
Our pride remembers it forever.'**
Lord Chesterfield, *Letters to His Son*

MY OWN RELATIONSHIPS over the decades offer a smorgasbord of barnies. There have been arguments with partners about my chocolate consumption in bed, my total indifference to housework and my strong disdain for cooking and for folding clothes. In all these heated discussions, a partner mistakenly thought it might help to tell me to calm down. And in every instance it had precisely the opposite effect.

Bickering that begins in a friendly, even comical way can easily descend into warfare. It might be over whether to put a tracker on each other's phone (er, no), one partner's habit of leaving dirty socks on the floor or hiding the remote control (annoying), or one of us being more skilled at parallel parking (me, obviously).

There are few phrases in the English language that are more incendiary than telling someone to 'calm down' during a fight. Whatever the dispute, the person who deploys the phrase had better armour up. Even my teenage sons, whom I love and adore more than life itself, say, 'Chillax, Mum,' which naturally riles me up.

Stephanie Yates-Anyabwile, a family marriage therapist, recommends people remove this phrase from their repertoire altogether. On her YouTube channel, she analyses couples fighting in films, points out areas where their arguments are constructive and where they are destructive, and suggests techniques to help de-escalate a disagreement. Yates-Anyabwile suggests resolving disputes when things are less tense and have cooled down. Using arguments as an opportunity to learn more about a partner's perspective instead of one-upping them is likely to achieve a better outcome.

Alain de Botton, in *The Course of Love*, says that couples rarely squabble over nothing, and that small issues are really large issues that have been overlooked. He brands disagreements as 'loose threads' that catch on fundamental differences in personalities. Most couples argue at some point. (If they do not, that is quite annoying for the rest of us.) Arguing can be healthy, but this depends on the scale, the topic and the ability to bounce back and apologise so problems do not fester. A good argument can help fortify a relationship if the issues are resolved.

Fighting with your partner breaks that 'us versus them' bond that gives you the ability to take on the world. You are angry with them and the universe. Petty grievances accumulate, secrets build up and bickering intensifies over seemingly small things as you grieve an alternative life you never pursued. DJ Fat Tony's Insta feed (@dj_fattony_) advises us to accept people for who they are but 'place them where they belong', instead of attempting to curate them into who you want them to be.

There are four things that can kill a relationship with military precision: contempt, sarcasm, stonewalling and – the biggest of them all – criticism. American psychologist John Gottman, whose work focuses on divorce prediction and marital stability, calls these the 'four horsemen'. Critical people generally believe they are giving helpful feedback, but we resist criticism because – unsurprisingly – we do not like being devalued. Gottman's analysis found that the optimal ratio for a healthy marriage was five positive comments for every negative one. Divorced couples ended up with a ratio of three positive comments for every four negative ones.

Compliments are easy to dish out when things are going well. When you hit a tricky patch in the marriage, it is easier to find fault with your partner and much more difficult to voice positive feedback. As Oscar Wilde is thought to have said, 'Criticism is the only reliable form of autobiography.' What he meant was that it gives more insight into the author of the criticism than its object. When criticism focuses on personality rather than behaviour, and when it includes 'the right way to do things', it serves only as a weapon of destruction. Feedback that produces positive change focuses on behaviour, is encouraging, respects the other's autonomy and includes offers to help.

What do the Stoics say?

Cato the Elder (234–149 BCE), also known as Cato the Censor, was a Roman statesman, soldier and historian whose philosophy shared some similarities with Stoic principles. If we all heeded these wise words of his, then we would rarely argue: 'I begin to speak only when I'm certain what I'll say isn't better left unsaid.' His sentiment was shared by Marcus Aurelius, who observed that unbridled anger is often more damaging to the angry person than the issue that caused the emotion.

If Seneca's spouse had left bills unpaid and told her husband to stick it up his backside when he asked what was for dinner, he would not have responded with anger. 'We shouldn't control our anger, but destroy it entirely,' he said, 'for what control is there for a thing that is fundamentally wicked?'

Arguments might give us momentary relief – like removing a cork will release built-up pressure – but they can leave behind emptiness, guilt, resentment and shame. And anger is contagious, allowing passion to overtake reason – the antithesis of stoicism. Seneca advised us to give anger space, and let the heat of an argument dissipate so that the 'fog that shrouds the mind may subside or become less thick'. He believed we must heal rather than seek revenge, because vengeance is a waste of precious time. And anger always outlasts hurt, he said.

Crucially, Stoicism recognises that resentment stems from suppressed emotions, and so it encourages introspection as an alternative path. Likewise, unless we can talk openly about a problem with our partner, we don't know what is going on, and this paves the way for our imagination to fill the gaps. Finding a partner who promotes harmony, self-control and support will help mitigate overreactions to unfavourable circumstances. Self-deprecating humour disarms insults and reduces the damage they inflict. Ultimately, the Stoic approach to relationships promotes greater understanding, transcending troubles and tackling anger through self-reflection.

A FINAL WORD FROM THE STOICS

'Remember that foul words or blows in themselves are no outrage, but your judgment that they are so. So when anyone makes you angry, know that it is your own thought that has angered you ... For if once you gain time and delay, you will find it easier to control yourself.'
Epictetus, *Enchiridion*

RULE 26
Be transparent
with money

'Money can't buy you happiness, but it does bring you
a more pleasant form of misery.'
Attributed to Spike Milligan

AS A UNIVERSITY STUDENT, I was commissioned as a market
researcher to carry out a survey inspired by the 1993 film *Indecent
Proposal*, in which a hard-up couple finds financial salvation when
Demi Moore's character agrees to spend the night with Robert
Redford, who pays her $1 million for her efforts. Unsurprisingly, the
arrangement leads to marital disharmony. My job was to ask randomly
selected people whether they would cheat for $1 million. All the men
said yes, absolutely – unlike the women I spoke to, who said no way.
As to what this means … who can say? But for the men I spoke to,
it's clear that money trumps monogamy.

The subject of money regularly polls as the number-one topic for
marital arguments. How many bags of clothing can you sneak into
the house undetected before your spouse sniffs your top and says it
smells new? Being skint is not a happy place to be because it limits
your freedom, and financial disclosure is an important feature of a
healthy relationship. A 2023 study by the Kelley School of Business at

Indiana University tracked 230 couples over two years, monitoring how they banked and how they felt about their relationship. It concluded that those with merged accounts reported higher levels of communality compared to those with separate or partially merged accounts.

Disagreements around finances can easily get swept under the carpet when a couple has wildly different views on managing money. But if left unchecked, they can take a scythe to the relationship. Especially if one partner is financially floundering while the other has conveniently failed to disclose their large savings stash. That can create enormous headaches, especially when shared property and kids are involved. Agreeing early on who pays what bill and how you will split the financial burden is so much better than having blow-ups over money down the track. In extreme cases, one partner might control the other's access to money, which can be a form of abuse.

Sharing expenses out of a joint account reduces the chance of arguments, but too much disclosure can also be limiting, as we all need our own money. It's about finding the right balance of trust and freedom. That's why it is so critical to have conversations early on about how to set up an egalitarian system for your shared finances that recognises both domestic and financial contributions to the partnership. A senior executive at a large global corporate once reminded me of the old adage that 'a man or woman is not a plan'. She strongly advocated for women who become mothers to maintain their careers, so they have the financial freedom to leave a relationship if they want or need to.

What do the Stoics say?

Marcus Aurelius believed humans were created for work, and not to huddle under the doona. This is good news for couples who want to share the load in building the family's wealth. Discipline, purpose and cooperation lay the groundwork for success. A joint bank account means you cannot sneak a Birkin bag into the house undetected.

RULE 26 Be transparent with money

The idea is to establish ground rules on money early. That may require both partners to compromise, which is fine as long as there is transparency and no power imbalance. Invoking the virtues of temperance and justice with finances will avert heated discussions over money. That means limiting spending sprees and adopting an agreed approach – which is easier said than done, given this is such a significant area of division among couples.

Balancing transparency with freedom is important. Stoic philosophy evolved at a time of legitimised slavery, the ultimate curtailment of freedom – and indeed Epictetus himself was enslaved by Nero's secretary. However, he believed that we are enslaved by our desires rather than by our circumstances. Money can also enslave us in a desire for more wealth, an obsession to control the spending habits of our partner or envy over the financial comfort achieved by our peers. These are internal thought processes, and so are within our control.

A FINAL WORD FROM THE STOICS
'And what is freedom, you ask? It means not being a slave to any circumstance, to any constraint, to any chance.'
Seneca, 'On Baiae and Morals'

RULE 27
Curse #blessed smug couples

> '*The world has grown so suspicious of anything that looks like a happily married life.* '
>
> Oscar Wilde, *Lady Windemere's Fan*

IT WAS A SATURDAY night and the following posts from friends appeared on social media.

> Happy 20th anniversary to my endless love, the hottest bloke I've ever laid eyes on let alone slept with, my beloved DILF. What a life we have filled with fun, laughter and rumpy pumpy. Looking forward to the next 20 years. I love you more than words can express. *#soblessed #loveofmylife #thankgodImnotsingle*

And this:

> Darling – thank you for the most wonderful 10 years of marriage – you are the wind beneath my wings, the sunshine in my life, my lover and best friend. I love sharing this crazy journey of love with you. *#blessedforever #hotspunk #Iloveyousomuch #notasingleloseranymore*

And this:

> Happy birthday to my husband Phil. You are the star to my satellite. You
> are the rock that I orbit around. Love you to the moon and back babe.
> *#blessed #soulmates*

There are people whose purpose in life is to make the rest of us in less
amorous situations feel bad. From the sidelines, it appears that they
breeze through their days with an abundance of love, money, time and
freedom in a trouble-free bubble of romance and adventure. But, as
my mother likes to say, 'Just you wait!' because you never know what's
around the corner.

That sounds like sour grapes, and it is. Even so, why would you post
such drivel on social media when your partner is sitting next to you
on the couch in trackies eating chips? Wouldn't it be easier to turn to
them and say, 'You are the rock I orbit around,' and spare the rest of us?
No one posts about the arguments they have over how much to feed the
cats, whether it is acceptable to spend money on a mirrored shoe rack
or who was responsible for denting the car.

Worse is calling your partner 'babe'. Many lovely, intelligent people
use this word. I asked some married friends their thoughts on 'babe'
and they said: 'We love it!' Then the husband said to his wife: 'Babe, can
you order me some spring rolls?' 'Sure, babe,' she said. Worse is 'baby'
or variants like 'bubba' and 'baba ganoush', terms of affection that
are meant to be healthier but are a bit revolting – rather like wearing
matching pyjamas with your beloved.

What do the Stoics say?

#luvmysexywife: *Cato the Elder once had Manilius, a Roman senator,
expelled from the Senate for embracing his wife in broad daylight while
his daughter was looking on. Cato claimed that he never embraced
his wife except after a loud clap of thunder, and he joked that Jupiter's*

thunder made him a happy man. At least he wasn't getting frisky with someone else's wife.

#Imananimal: *The Greeks were similarly down on public displays of affection, adopting the Roman view that PDAs exhibited an almost animalistic lack of self-control.*

#lifenotworthlivingwithoutyoubabe: *The Romans knew how to express love and sorrow in a far more extreme fashion than Instagram allows. Porcia Catonis, the daughter of Cato the Younger, was devoted to her husband, Marcus Junius Brutus. When Mark Antony found Brutus lying dead, he ordered the body to be wrapped in his expensive robes; afterwards, on hearing that the robes had been stolen, he put the thief to death. The ashes of Brutus were sent home to his mother, Servilia. Porcia was so distraught that she ended her life by swallowing live coals from the fire.*

A FINAL WORD FROM THE STOICS

'Don't be prideful with any excellence that is not your own ... when you behave conformably to nature in reaction to how things appear, you will be proud with reason; for you will take pride in some good of your own.'
Epictetus, *Enchiridion*

RULE 28
Don't expect perfection

'Nothing is an unmixed blessing.'
Horace, *Odes*

GEORGE HAS BEEN with Toby for two decades, a milestone he attributes to not expecting perfection. Compromise, honesty and trust formed the trifecta that has maintained their monogamy and longevity. 'There's a level where you have to be okay with what you've got,' George says. 'Don't expect perfection. Some people are so aspirational and never happy with what they've got. Sometimes, you have to be happy to be okay with okay.'

George was 29 when he met Toby, and understood by then what he was looking for in a partner. His only other previous long-term relationship was with a woman at a time when he had begun to question his sexuality. 'I was coasting along with her and had thoughts of Arnold Schwarzenegger when we had sex,' he said. 'We did musical theatre together and shopped for homewares – I should have known then.' He had a few dalliances – with a male tour guide on a US Contiki tour and another bloke who looked like a character from the Blue Oyster Bar in the first *Police Academy* film – before meeting Toby.

Author Alain de Botton in *The Course of Love* cautions that we all have appalling traits, so it is best not to expect perfection but instead settle for good enough. He argues that our friends know more about us than we do, and ex-lovers are more fluent in our flaws. In order to have a fulfilling relationship, though, we must know ourselves. The people we love will inevitably disappoint us, De Botton warns, but the trick is to recognise that every one of us is a mix of good and not so good, and not to run away at the first sign of trouble.

Psychotherapist Esther Perel explores the tension between erotic and domestic expectations in her book *Mating in Captivity: Unlocking Erotic Intelligence*, wisely advising us to manage our expectations. 'Never have we expected more from our intimate relationships, and never have we crumbled under the weight of so many expectations,' she says. Historically, marriage was more like a business transaction, and the romantic expectations of men and women were lower compared to modern times. The trick these days, Esther believes, is to diversify our expectations: 'Don't ask one person to give you what a village should give you,' she advises.

Jane Austen explored the theme of realistic expectations in *Mansfield Park*, where the protagonist, Fanny Price, ends up with the steady bloke and not the exciting one. She is sent to live with her rich extended family because her family is too poor to keep her, and is subsequently treated like Cinderella. She ends up unrequitedly loving the only person who shows her some kindness, her elder cousin, Edmund Bertram. When she is 17, the good-looking, superficial and rich Henry and Mary Crawford move into the neighbourhood and cause drama. Henry unsuccessfully colludes with his sister to make Fanny fall in love with him for their amusement. In the end, Fanny and Edmund end up together.

Perhaps being treated so poorly by the broader family gave Fanny insight into Henry's flippant and hollow overtures, and so she waited for the dependable Edmund. Though it must have been frustrating when Edmund became smitten for a time with Mary. Personally, I'd have chucked them both. In any case, the story reinforces the value of having realistic expectations. Had Fanny ended up with the philandering Henry, then her life would have been in turmoil.

What do the Stoics say?

The Stoics focused on self-improvement rather than on the improvement of others, as no one can be forced to change. Marcus Aurelius experienced this at first hand through his errant son, Commodus, who was far from perfect. We have to accept that everyone has their faults, and we must work at improving our own. When we do so, those around us can be positively impacted as we work on cultivating the Stoic virtues. Marcus's wife, Faustina, who was also his first cousin, was reputed to have had affairs with gladiators and others, so it's inevitable that their marriage was complex and imperfect, but this did not stop him adoring her, both in life and after she died. Though rumours of the alleged affairs were likely fuelled by Marcus's political opponents to destabilise his regime.

A relationship that starts in the haze of a perfect love will inevitably change as the two people within it change. It exists in an imperfect world, where we experience demands on our attention, encounter misaligned values and must make complex decisions. Expecting our partner to be perfect is futile. 'Remember: you shouldn't be surprised that a fig tree produces figs, nor the world what it produces,' Marcus said. 'A good doctor isn't surprised when his patients have fevers, or a helmsman when the wind blows against him.'

It is by striving to live a virtuous life, rather than by demanding perfection, that we can achieve the best relationship possible for ourselves and our partner.

A FINAL WORD FROM THE STOICS
'It is great folly not to part with your own faults which is possible, but to try instead to escape from other people's faults, which is impossible.
Marcus Aurelius, *Meditations*

RULE 28 Don't expect perfection

RULE 29
Live on the edge – but not too close to it

'Life is either a daring adventure, or nothing.'
Helen Keller

SOME RELATIONSHIPS ARE great because you are living on the outer ring of your comfort zone, trying new and exciting things all the time. Travelling, surfing, skiing, going to gigs or the opera. It's probably unfair to compare life before kids, mortgages, careers and financial obligations with life after those things crash into your life, but we all do it anyway.

Psychotherapist Esther Perel advises couples to regularly go outside their comfort zone. New and exciting activities create intensity and demand risk-taking, and these can keep the spark in a relationship alive. Too much challenge and change, though, can veer into chaos. Striking a balance between exploration, curiosity and stability is important so long as there is shared growth. Perel's message is that 'if you don't change or grow, you fossilise and you die'.

'Relationships help you become who you are,' Perel says. We may love many people over a lifetime, and while many of us are searching for a love story, she advises that we view it as a life story. A love story comprises many ingredients and values, such as interdependence or self-reliance. Rifts arise from a clash of values – for instance, if one partner likes to bring people to the house while the other shuns socialising. A lack of alignment can cause relationships to rupture. Calibrating their expectations and expecting disappointment helps people navigate setbacks. Critical is how we repair cracks and respond to what psychologist John Gottman describes as bids for connection or gestures to show you care.

If you really want to live on the edge, try leaving the kitchen cupboards open, abandoning a half-eaten sandwich on the bench, or mopping the floor with your feet while wearing socks. These take courage if you are with someone who is finnicky about housework. While they might be time savers, they make life more difficult when you live with a neat freak.

Or, as documented in *The New Yorker*, take relationship advice from your aunt, who's been married too many times to count on one hand. She is full of helpful advice, such as to aim low. 'Never trust a Gary,' she says. 'I will not be elaborating on this. He knows what he did, that little weasel.' Be understanding of what your potential spouse is going through. 'If he has a latex allergy, develop one, too. If he has a demanding schedule and can't commit to plans, make sure that you're available all the time.' Also, don't go to bed angry – 'stay up and fight ... You'll get used to the lack of sleep, which will allow you to annihilate your sweetheart at the next morning's breakfast fight.'

What do the Stoics say?

For the Stoics, a key theme was achieving growth by overcoming challenges. Marcus Aurelius said that difficulties strengthen our minds and that obstacles advance our actions. Epictetus believed that comfort is the enemy of progress. He wrote in Discourses, *'It is difficulties that show what men are.' Seneca, in his* Moral Essays to Lucilius, *said, 'Valor withers without adversity.'*

The Japanese concept of wabi-sabi *sees perfection in imperfection.*

It encourages acceptance of the transient and imperfect nature of things, a concept that is similar in spirit to Stoicism but well outside the comfort zone of perfectionists.

Practising discomfort helps us cultivate virtue. Pushing ourselves beyond our natural inclinations opens us to experiences that can change us for the better. A recent study by Harvard researchers concluded that it's not the situation itself that causes us emotional turmoil, it's how we think about it. That's no surprise, says writer Meredith Kunz, who blogs as The Stoic Mom. *Stoics have known this for more than 2000 years.*

Our concept of perfection doesn't exist in reality. As Marcus Aurelius points out, things are impermanent: they are constantly changing and decaying. All we can hope for is to move in the right direction, which is that indicated by virtue.

A FINAL WORD FROM THE STOICS
'Ask not that events should happen as you will, but let your will be that events should happen as they do, and you shall have peace.'
Epictetus, *Enchiridion*

RULE 29 Live on the edge – but not too close to it

RULE 30
Prioritise yourself

'Self-sacrifice enables us to sacrifice
other people without blushing.'
George Bernard Shaw, *Man and Superman*

IF THE IDEA of being apart from your beloved makes you feel sick,
then you may be onto a good thing. If the idea of being apart is
something you look forward to, maybe not.

There's a gulf between putting yourself first at the expense of
others and prioritising your own needs. Kindness and selfishness
are not opposing forces. It is possible to prioritise yourself and still
care for others deeply. There is no contradiction between loving
others and meeting your own needs. Putting yourself last, keeping
tight-lipped about what you want and letting resentment bubble up
is as bad as putting everyone else last. Ideally, let your partner know
your boundaries before a limit has been reached and they unwittingly
overstep them.

Depleting your soul by being selfless can leave you burnt out
at work and on the home front. Humanist psychologist Scott Barry
Kaufman argues that healthy selfishness is an act of self-love. It is
about enforcing boundaries and saying no in order to conserve your
time, energy and spirit while still deeply caring for others. This
healthy selfishness is associated with wellbeing, life satisfaction and

psychological adaptability, self-compassion and a sense of pride in response to achievements. The Dalai Lama says that 'wise selfishness' focuses on the personal benefits of helping others, but not at the expense of your own needs.

Overextending ourselves is the opposite of boundary setting, which is a critical life skill. Our early family relationships can sabotage our relationships later in life. An overbearing mother or a father who showed little interest might shape a need in us for validation. Conversely, a happy, comfortable childhood might leave some ill-prepared for challenges in a relationship.

Couples, too, sometimes need to prioritise themselves over the demands that others place on them. Nick and Bot had been together for more than 15 years, but in the first few years, Bot didn't reveal to his family that Nick was his partner, anticipating a lack of cultural acceptance. Bot's parents lived in Vietnam and assumed Nick was his landlord – a ruse the couple went along with. They prioritised their relationship, keeping at a distance from a community that seemingly did not support their union. However, Bot's siblings and brother-in-law supported them after they went on to marry. They attribute the longevity of their 15-year relationship to good communication, not assuming they can read each other's mind, and the freedom to do things apart as well as together.

What do the Stoics say?

One common criticism of Stoicism is that it is self-centred rather than outward-looking, but this is a misunderstanding of its approach. Stoics focus on the self in order to assess what is within their sphere of control, because improving themselves is also good for those around them. If you are living a virtuous life, you are working for your own benefit as well as the benefit of others.

Marcus Aurelius believed that people existed for the sake of one another, and that cooperation was essential to success. At the same

RULE 30 Prioritise yourself

time, he held that we strengthen our own soul by being strict on ourselves and tolerant of others. Epictetus asked whether 'you would be willing to die for your country, and buy the safety of all your fellow-citizens at the price of your own; whether you would offer your neck not only with patience, but also with gladness. If you would do this, there is no other good in your eyes. For you are giving up everything in order to acquire this good.'

Stoicism is anything but selfish — but the cause must be worthy. This does not apply to self-sacrifice that is demanded of you, perhaps for reasons that are not virtuous. You are not a slave to others, but contributing to the common good is a worthy goal.

A FINAL WORD FROM THE STOICS

'The Universe, too, loves to create what is to be.
Therefore I say to the Universe: "Your love is mine."'
Marcus Aurelius, *Meditations*

RULE 31
Remember that you can be happy or you can be right

**'Righteousness cannot be born
until self-righteousness is dead.'**
Bertrand Russell, *Justice in War-Time*

FOR SOME, THERE is nothing more appealing than people who just go with the flow. They face the ups and downs of life with a sense of equanimity and don't sweat the small stuff. They embrace uncertainty, unafraid of a bit of disorder and chaos. At the other end of the spectrum are the people who require structure and need everything to be a certain way, and are upset when it isn't. Some even feel it appropriate to have control over their beloved, when really they have no more right to it than to appoint themselves Prime Minister.

Pointing out your partner's flaws and the reasons why they should adopt everything you say, do and think will do nothing but strain relations, build resentment and wound a partnership. 'You can be happy or you can be right,' a couples counsellor once told me.

'Can't you be both?' I asked.

'No,' she said firmly. 'They are mutually exclusive.'

Poet Mary Oliver understood the futility of believing your own hype. 'Let me keep my distance, always, from those who think they have the answers,' she said. She believed the mysteries of this world were 'too marvelous to be understood' and explored how gravity worked; for her, poetry provided a source of comfort. She advised distance from those who believe to always have the answers to the unknowable mysteries of the world.

Our behavioural and thinking patterns are strongly influenced by our childhood experiences and internalised beliefs. 'Reaction formation' is a psychological mechanism we sometimes use to confront our own painful feelings of inadequacy. We deliver withering putdowns to elevate ourselves and create a sense of superiority. This stems from a need to be in control of people and situations to compensate for feeling out of control.

According to *Psychology Today*, the need to control often manifests as a need to be right. For people who are emotionally attached to being correct, any idea, thought or action to the contrary must be wrong. This response merely causes the rest of us to suffer. Indeed, asserting one's correctness over others can be a form of mental enslavement.

What do the Stoics say?

When Marcus Aurelius was emperor of Rome, it was a time of war, famine, treachery and disease, and yet he was renowned for his openness to advice. After listening, he had the good judgement and wisdom to distinguish between good and bad counsel, while acknowledging his own imperfections.

He believed that criticism from other people should not be accepted uncritically, advising us to 'separate from yourself ... all that troubles you in the future, all that as part of the bodily envelope or natural spirit attaches to you without your will, and all that the external circumfluent vortex whirls round, so that your mind power [is] freed from the chain of necessity [and] lives purified and released by itself'.

He was not discouraged by criticism from others, and in fact welcomed constructive feedback as a learning opportunity. But if criticism of us has no validity, he believed, then we must not be discouraged. He took responsibility for his actions and trained himself to ignore self-righteous criticism, attributing the hurt people caused him on their own character and actions, not his own. 'What is done to me is ordained by nature, what I do by my own.'

Criticism may be valid if constructive; if not, it is best to ignore it and understand what is fuelling the desire for a verbal jab. Likewise, take care in dishing out your own advice to your loved one – it may not be the path to happiness.

A FINAL WORD FROM THE STOICS

'Don't regard what anyone says of you, for this, after all, is no concern of yours. How long, then, will you put off thinking yourself worthy of the highest improvements and follow the distinctions of reason?'

Epictetus, *Enchiridion*

RULE 31 Remember that you can be happy or you can be right

RULE 32
Keep the flames
of desire burning

'Personally, I know nothing about sex
as I've always been married.'

Zsa Zsa Gabor

THERE IS NOTHING less sexy than being in the trenches of parenthood,
with a backstabbing boss and a towering pile of bills thrown in for
good measure. It's easy to let the romantic side of a relationship
slide. However, a sex drought can also mask cracks in a relationship.
Whether or not you have kids, keeping the sexual flame alight requires
spontaneity, dedication and commitment. Because, as a relationship
counsellor once said to me, if you are not having sex, then you might as
well be sister and brother (eww).

The great sex drought has even hit the love capital of the world, with
The Guardian reporting that the French have lost their va-va-voom.
Nearly a quarter of French people aged 18–69 said they had not had
sex in the previous 12 months. The French Institute of Public Opinion
suggested it may be a social correction following a more lustful
previous generation, or perhaps scrolling has replaced sex for some.

For those still on the wagon, sex is thoroughly lovely – until you
have an argument, or a child that needs feeding, or a bill that needs

paying, or when you're just tired from work, family and life. All of a sudden, sex becomes much less lovely. So, in an effort to spice things up, you buy a pair of edible underwear and give it to your partner for Christmas. They unwrap it and look at it with a mixture of confusion and disdain, before asking whether you kept the receipt. Such a response can undermine your confidence – but, as with everything in an otherwise good relationship, this can be rectified.

One sure-fire way of keeping the bedroom fires burning, according to another *Guardian* article, is to pick up the toilet brush and get cleaning. Countries where men and women share chores tend to have more children, and more children definitely suggests you've had more sex. According to Japan's *Nikkei* newspaper, in both France and Norway men tend to do more around the house and also have more children. Japanese and South Korean women, by contrast, are still picking up the domestic slack and having fewer kids.

Sex and communication are inexorably linked, and help couples stay in step with one another. Lengthy sex droughts that couples fail to address can derail a relationship, because they may mask a festering issue and fuel resentment, or can be weaponised during arguments rather than thoughtfully and honestly discussed. Even better is to address desire levels and sex preferences well before the drought hits – how many times a week, month or year, and what time of day is optimal (i.e. not when you are dog-tired). Do you need to buy one of those sex position books to keep things adventurous? Or perhaps arrange weekends away sans kids and family duties? Either way, it's a good habit to include sex in the conversational repertoire so that it doesn't become a vexed topic.

What do the Stoics say?

At first glance, the Stoics had little to say about sex – and much of what they did say was about prostitution and sexual relations with slaves. But Marcus Aurelius encouraged us to 'love the people with whom fate brings you together, but do so with all your heart' – a sentiment we now know can be fulfilled so long as your partner pitches in and cleans the toilet and folds the laundry.

Early Stoics such as Zeno and Chrysippus were even in favour of polyamory, in an attempt to win paternal affection and protection for the family. The ancient Stoics regarded erotic love primarily as a means of securing interpersonal relationships within the community.

Marcus Aurelius cautioned against allowing a relationship to slowly slip away, urging people to live it fully every day, and that would likely include in the bedroom, although he did not specify. Sexual misalignment and lack of intimacy are awkward and fraught subjects to discuss as a couple for fear of rejection, yet intimacy is often the foundation of a healthy relationship, and discussing sexual desire and issues early sets up a relationship for success.

One imagines that the Stoics were masters at having awkward conversations. They taught the virtues of emotional control, clear expression, active listening and empathy to navigate tricky subjects. Famously, Zeno said: 'The reason why we have two ears and only one mouth is that we may listen the more and talk the less.' The Stoics encouraged self-reflection and openness, which may be the pillars of a happy ending for both of you.

A FINAL WORD FROM THE STOICS

'We receive comfort, even at a distance, from those we love, but then it is light and faint; whereas, presence and conversation touch us to the quick, especially if we find the man we love to be such a person as we wish.'

Seneca, 'The Blessings of Friendship'

RULE 32 Keep the flames of desire burning

RULE 33
Beware temptation

**'Watch and pray, that ye not enter into temptation:
the spirit indeed is willing but the flesh is weak.'**
Gospel of St Matthew, 26:41

BEING ATTRACTED TO other people is one of the biggest threats to
any stable relationship. Temptation is everywhere – and, increasingly,
online. Even more so in the world of celebrity, where egos are huge,
senses of entitlement rife and money plentiful. Tiger Woods allegedly
bedded a dizzying number of women while married, which would
be impossible for most of us civilians juggling full-time work with
families. Brad Pitt must rue the day he got together with Angelina Jolie
while married to Jennifer Aniston. Jude Law had a dalliance with the
nanny while in a relationship with Sienna Miller, and Hugh Grant was
arrested after cheating on Liz Hurley.

The most shocking part is how shocked we are each time these
stories are publicised given cheating has been going on since the dawn
of humans. While it is impossible to get accurate data, cheating is likely
more widespread than we would like to believe. About 60 per cent of
men and 45 per cent of women are estimated to have cheated in some
form during their marriage. Some 70 per cent of all marriages will
experience a physical or emotional affair at some point.

In the TV thriller *Doctor Foster*, a female doctor finds a blonde hair on her husband's scarf, resulting in stalking and revenge cheating that permeates a community. How you would react if you discovered your partner had cheated is a common scenario couples like to stress-test early in their relationship. Some vow to castrate their male partners; others say they would seek revenge. (Really, the best revenge is to no longer care about revenge.) Others say they would be hurt but would move on with their life. For some, the longer the relationship, the more tolerant they become – but the reverse can also be true.

British actress Amy Nuttall reconciled with her husband Andrew Buchan, who had strayed, on the proviso he adhere to seven strict rules, including no contact with the woman he had an affair with and full phone access. She introduced the 777 approach, which means going on a date every seven days, a night away every seven weeks and a holiday together every seven months.

The rights and wrongs of infidelity can be complicated, and love does not adhere to any limitations such as relationship status, gender or geography. Cressida met her wife, Mia, eight years ago when they were both in unfulfilling relationships with other people – Cressida with a man and Mia with a woman. They developed feelings for one another and both realised they needed to end their respective relationships to start something new. This caused drama among their friends and family members who disapproved of the overlap. But Cressida felt sexually unfulfilled with men and took the leap despite having not strictly ended her first relationship.

Infidelity at the tail end of a relationship – sometimes called 'cheating without cheating' – is probably more commonplace than people admit. And we can be unwittingly unfaithful without even knowing it. Too much focus on another person, no matter how innocent, may constitute 'micro-cheating'. These are small actions that indicate someone has crossed a line, such as having private online conversations. Secrecy and deception are the giveaways.

Sometimes we might leap at shadows or overreact to something that isn't there. Even so, we are entitled to an open discussion about our concerns, and to expect some reassurance from our partner to address a problem.

A relationship is unlikely to emerge in the same state after an affair, a study published in *Psychological Science* concluded. But it remained inconclusive as to whether relationship problems flow from infidelity or whether cheating on your partner is a symptom of a troubled relationship. Bruno Kirby's character believed the latter when he said, in *When Harry Met Sally*, 'Marriages don't break up on account of infidelity. It's just a symptom that something else is wrong.'

What do the Stoics say?

Sexual morality in the time of the Stoics was simply different from that of the 21st-century Western world. The Stoics did not agree on the use of prostitutes and sleeping with one's slaves and servants, but in the time of Zeno polygamy was accepted, while Marcus Aurelius saw sex as primarily for procreation within marriage.

The Roman poet Horace tells of the senator and moralist Cato seeing a young man coming out of a brothel; Cato congratulates him for exercising his lusts there rather than with some man's wife. Epictetus advised that we should 'avoid impurity to the upmost of our ability before marriage', as it is 'not a game. It gives rise to very real enduring emotional and practical consequences'. However, he added: 'An active sex life within a framework of personal commitment augments the integrity of the people involved and is part of a flourishing life.'

Fast-forward to a time of contraception, late marriage and even later childbearing, and you would think we might be more liberal in our views on unsanctioned infidelity. But if the celebrity stories are to be believed, it continues to wreak havoc on relationships. Betrayal contravenes the cardinal virtue of justice, unless there is an agreement to stray.

RULE 33 Beware temptation

Temperance reduces lustful impulses through self-restraint, a habit Epictetus espoused. Resisting temptation is part of a Stoic framework that helps us make wise decisions for the greater good. The Stoics encouraged giving thoughtful consideration to decisions, including with whom we sleep, as more fruitful outcomes come from intelligent decision-making. A delicate walk of shame after a late-night hook-up is fine for someone not looking for meaning, but disappointing for those seeking a deeper emotional bond.

A FINAL WORD FROM THE STOICS

'If laying aside that fidelity for which we were born, we form designs against the wife of our neighbour, what do we do? What else but destroy and ruin – what? Fidelity, honour, and the sanctity of manners. Only these? And do we not ruin friendship, neighbourhood, our country? In what rank do we then place ourselves?'
Epictetus, *Discourses*

RULE 34
Stay or go – but not both

'Wishing each other, not divorced, but dead;
They lived respectably as man and wife.'
Lord Byron, *Don Juan*

WHEN YOU RETURN from work on a dark Monday evening to a damp rental flat and slather a mouldy cracker with peanut butter because that's the only food in your pantry, it is tempting to focus on the things you gave up when your relationship ended. You wonder what led to the end of that era of your life.

As you think back, you remember your partner as a carefree, breezy, spontaneous person who dragged you out of bed at 1 am to watch a laser light show in the city before drinking vodka jelly shots on a Ferris wheel by the beach. You do not remember the prolonged silences, punctuated only by your partner snapping at you for leaving too many cat tunnels in the hallway, or the strategically different times you went to bed to avoid romance, or the fact that you would rather cuddle the family hamster.

This is what's known as 'euphoric recall': the tendency to remember past events in a positive way, regardless of what actually happened. It can motivate us to revive a past relationship, even when there were very good reasons for splitting. Indeed, some couples remain locked in each other's gravitational pull, breaking up and then getting together again repeatedly.

No couple is more famous for this than movie stars Elizabeth Taylor and Richard Burton – or 'Dickenliz', as they were known. They were both married to other people when they first got together on the set of the 1962 blockbuster *Cleopatra*. They dumped their spouses and remained together for 13 years, before a trifecta of drugs, booze and infidelity resulted in divorce. A year later, they remarried in Botswana, but things lasted only another year before imploding again. Taylor said she did not 'want to be that much in love ever again … I gave everything away … my soul, my being, everything.' The moral of their on again, off again relationship is that love alone is sometimes not enough.

Amazingly, 10–15 per cent of divorcing couples reconcile, according to US marriage data. Some 6 per cent go as far as remarrying – and, remarkably, those couples then have a divorce rate lower than that of the general population. This is probably because breaking up and divorcing is so terrible that to repeat such an atrocious experience and resume eating limp lettuce for dinner would, for most people, be unthinkable.

The world of business offers a useful analogy for people embarking on a relationship, according to *The Atlantic*. It says the sweet spot for an enduring romantic partnership is somewhere closer to a start-up than a merger – a new venture between two experienced founders who are not yet set in their ways, rather than the joining of two existing companies trying to negotiate between their entrenched behaviours.

The most common reason couples reconcile and get back together is that they resolve the problems that initially troubled them, whether that was a lack of intimacy, financial stress or a lack of attention. Ultimately, though, you cannot have one foot on the train and the other on the platform – it is either all in or all out.

What do the Stoics say?

Relationships are messy and complicated, and are generally ruled by the heart, not the head. But some rational thinking can help rein in the emotions that cloud our judgement. For the Stoics, a decision about whether to return to a previous partner would be determined by logic and wisdom.

A saying commonly misattributed to both Albert Einstein and Mark Twain holds that 'insanity is doing the same thing over and over and expecting a different result'. If the reasons your relationship ended have not been addressed, then there is no cause to think it should be any different a second time around, regardless of how attractive your ex now appears, or how much you fear being alone. If you have both tackled the relationship's failings, however, then a reconciliation may be worth pursuing.

In the same way that ruminating on the past is pointless, as the past cannot be changed, selectively recalling positive events can be damaging. We should strive to see things as they truly are, not as we would like them to be. The Stoics believed that since we can only act in the present moment, that is where our focus should be. Decisions are better based on the facts as they are now, not on what happened, good or bad, in an unchangeable past.

A FINAL WORD FROM THE STOICS

'You must plan your life, one action at a time, and be content if each acquires its own end as best it can; and that it should acquire its end, no one at all can prevent you.'

Marcus Aurelius, *Meditations*

RULE 34 Stay or go – but not both

PART THREE
BREAKING UP

'For his pleasure he got married.
On his thinking it over he got divorced.'

Sumerian proverb

DOs & DON'Ts

LISTEN TO: 'Ain't No Pleasing You', Chas & Dave; 'We Are Never Ever Getting Back Together', Taylor Swift; 'Que Sera Sera', Doris Day; 'So Long', ABBA

DON'T LISTEN TO: 'Revenge', Pink featuring Eminem; 'Don't Wanna See Your Face Again', John Butler Trio; 'She Hates Me', Puddle of Mudd

EAT: Chocolate, cheese, caramel popcorn, chips, triple brie, buckets of chocolate fudge ice-cream

DON'T EAT: Steamed vegetables (this is no time for diets)

DRINK: Anything

DON'T DRINK: Everything

WATCH: *Marriage Story*; *Bridget Jones's Diary*

DON'T WATCH: *Misery*; *The Shining*; *The Lodge*

READ: *Tiny Beautiful Things: Advice on Love and Life from Dear Sugar* by Cheryl Strayed; *Rising Strong* by Brené Brown; *Us* by David Nicholls

DON'T READ: *The Art of War* by Sun Tzu; *Stay or Leave* by Beverley Stone (if you're reading this book, you might as well leave)

What breaks up a relationship is not always one big thing, but the unspoken smaller grievances that build up and cause irreparable damage. Isolated incidents may seem harmless and trivial, but an accumulation of them can be destabilising. Just because you've been with someone a long time does not mean that everything is humming along nicely. There may have been deep-seated issues that you both developed strategies to work around rather than confront head on. Those who address the issues and end up parting ways show immense courage.

Some say getting over a break-up takes half as long as a relationship – which is bad news for those who have been married for decades. In any case, most people seem to take a couple of years to course-correct and rebuild a functional relationship with their ex. Unless, of course, the ex is a simmering, seething, uncooperative ball of resentment who puts a padlock on the family home as part of a mission to make your life a misery and bleed you dry. Best to binge-eat chocolate until you fall into a sugar coma, or a family bag of salt and vinegar chips that leaves your tongue feeling like it's been covered in sandpaper. You can reconnect with reality when you're feeling more in control.

Take the higher ground, get professional support and adopt a Stoic mindset. Remember that shoddy behaviour from an ex merely confirms that the break-up was necessary.

Some may take sides, tilt their heads in sympathy and treat you like a leper for being single. The Stoics say change is about losing something old and gaining something new – like a more suitable partner. Pets, kids, friends and family can all be tremendous supports during this transition, although family can also be the opposite. Surround yourself with people who are spiritually nourishing, and make sure you eat lots of chocolate, listen to good music and watch comfort films before you re-enter the jungle of love.

RULE 35
Accept change

'Change does not come without inconvenience,
even from worse to better.'

Samuel Johnson, *A Dictionary of the English Language*

PIGEONS MAY HAVE a brain the size of a bean, but these birds can teach humans a lot about love. They feel it profoundly, protect their loved ones at the expense of their own safety and grieve when they die. Just like with humans, though, avian love can also turn sour. Birds can have spats, especially if they are migratory birds that travel thousands of kilometres. Great blue herons have a divorce rate of 100 per cent because they migrate over 3000 kilometres. That is, they brutally replace their living partner with another mid-flight, because they no longer give them what they need. Love's ubiquity is felt across generations, oceans and species. No wonder it sends us all a bit crazy.

Separation can leave you shrouded in a pall of grief and shock. The flaws that fractured the relationship in the first place are magnified by a factor of five, and really nothing anyone says or does can resolve them. Endings bring with them attachments to property and the flotsam of your life you once shared. Grief can shackle you and prevent you from moving forward. But endings need not be seen as failures. They are an opportunity to redefine what your relationship and family look like, and maybe even forge a better path.

But no matter how nice your ex-spouse may be, divorce is inevitably a protracted shitshow. Over time, though, it becomes slightly less horrible. The whole process is non-linear in that things get incrementally better, but can be easily derailed. It's a fragile ecosystem that must be delicately managed. Edgar Allan Poe cautioned that 'years of love have been forgot / in the hatred of a minute'. If your ex transforms into a psycho once you pull the pin and weaponises the family, the kids and even the in-laws against you, you're in for a rocky ride. And no matter how supportive your married friends and family are while you navigate the horrors of dismantling a marriage, no one can truly appreciate what you're going through – other than those who have also been through divorce. A separation impacts your home, your children, your extended family and friends, your work and your finances. It extends its tentacles into every aspect of your life. Some friends and family will be pillars of strength, whereas others make it all about them or side with your ex.

Celebrities have the wider problem of their smash-ups being spread all over the tabloids. Tom Cruise's ex Katie Holmes pulled off her divorce with *Mission Impossible*–like military precision. Her seamless exit involved moving into a new apartment, switching numbers and cutting all communications with Cruise. Kevin Costner pulled no punches, publicly insisting that his wife, Christine Baumgartner, exit the marital home when their marriage went belly-up. But British actor Ioan Gruffudd's bust-up from wife Alice Evans takes the cake. After he found love elsewhere, she kept the world informed via Twitter of every detail of their hot mess of a break-up, burned through her share of the proceeds from the separation and publicly announced that she would be forced to work at Starbucks.

Sometimes, people who were once an ideal match grow apart, but this does not erase the good parts of a relationship. It's a tenet of Stoicism that the past can't be changed. Although we sometimes forget it, that's equally true of the positive parts of a relationship. Those good

STOIC IN LOVE

times that happened should not be rewritten in the harsh light of later, less kind events.

What do the Stoics say?

When we're in the heat of a break-up, Stoic philosophy can remind us that what has gone before is now unalterable. The unwritten history of any relationship will have a mixture of good and bad times. Fear of the future can be debilitating but is equally pointless. The only time to concern yourself with is the present. Some horrors will have passed, never to return, and perhaps others await – but so do better times. We can only deal with things that are within our power.

Change is inevitable. 'The universe is change; our life is what our thoughts make it,' Marcus Aurelius said. Epictetus spoke of 'the chief test of all – "Is it concerned with what is in our power or with what is not in our power?" And if it is concerned with what is not in our power, be ready with the answer that it is nothing to you.'

Do not worry about a future that may never occur, nor the good and bad times in an unalterable past. Focus on making the right decisions in the present moment.

A FINAL WORD FROM THE STOICS

'Two elements must therefore be rooted out once and for all – the fear of future suffering, and the recollection of past suffering; since the latter no longer concerns me, and the former concerns me not yet.'
Seneca, 'On the Healing Power of the Mind'

RULE 35 Accept change

RULE 36
Celebrate singledom

'How sweet is harmless solitude!
What can its joys control?
Tumults and noise may not intrude,
To interrupt the soul.'

Mary Mollineux, 'Solitude'

A DIVORCED FRIEND, Rob, had recently partnered with Daisy, and they invited 100 people over for a Christmas party at the gargantuan house they bought together to accommodate the five kids they shared between them. The invitation was an elaborate animation that revealed the names of the guests invited:

Binky & Cam	Paola & Paul
Jan & Jez	Me
Alex & Adam	Kerry & Peter
Liz & Nick	Et cetera ...

Basically, it was a party of couples – and me, a freshly separated single parent. There was a live band, an illuminated pool with a viewing platform from the basement, and a couch that cost so much money no one was allowed to sit on it with a drink. The hosts were friendly and happy: having both been through the horrors of divorce, they understandably wanted to celebrate their good fortune in finding love again.

First up, Mark complimented me on ageing well and asked whether I had considered 'late-in-life lesbianism'.

'Er, no,' I replied. 'Have you?'

Another couple, Tom and Gia, asked where my partner was. I said I no longer had one, prompting a synchronised head tilt and pout before they said they were sorry for me.

As with everything in life, fortune plays a significant role in the unexpected twists and turns of our romantic lives. One minute you are loved up and posting on social media about how #blessed you are for your #soulmateinlife who can do no wrong. The next you find a suspicious text on their phone and discover that they don't really travel for work but have a wife and three kids on the other side of town (not in my case, I should add).

Being fresh from a break-up turns you into an immediate threat to the partnerships of others. That means that, at parties such as these, you need to rein in playful conversation in case the person you are flirting with is attached. Some people patrol their partner like a Border Force official, hooking their arm around their spouse whenever they detect a potential threat.

But flying solo is not all bad. You can watch your comfort film on repeat whenever you want. Showering is optional (at least for a while). Chocolate for breakfast and dinner is underrated. You can clean and wash up at your leisure – or not. There is no need to ever tread on eggshells or negotiate who uses the bathroom first, or interrogate why they left sodden towels on the floor and the toilet in a questionable state.

Life as part of a couple does not guarantee emotional calm and stability any more than single life does, but the ability to enjoy solitude can transform being single from good to great. There's a good case for flying solo, at least for a while, as hooking up on the rebound is notoriously bad for producing a long-lasting relationship. Singledom gives us freedom and a chance for self-improvement. It can also offer a welcome interlude between relationships – the chance to take stock, adjust course and really think about what we want out of a relationship.

What do the Stoics say?

The Stoics believed in retaining power over their own lives and destinies within the sphere of their control. Attachment for the sake of it, or for social conformity, would doubtless be frowned upon. To the Stoics, being in control of your life was a virtue. Far better to be single than in a bad relationship. And if you must end a relationship, it is best to do so with the goal of fairness and justice for all parties. Marcus Aurelius championed the benefits of solitude, viewing the soul as an 'untroubled retreat'.

In his letters, Seneca tells Lucilius about the benefits of quietude in order to study effectively. He forced his mind to concentrate and prevented it from straying to the bedlam outside – 'for of what benefit is a quiet neighbourhood, if our emotions are in an uproar?'

Marcus Aurelius stated that, 'Men seek retreats for themselves, houses in the country, sea-shores, and mountains.' But that solace could instead be found anywhere by retiring 'into his own soul.' Such solace isn't dependent on being with another, but can be found within ourselves. After a long relationship, being single can be a scary prospect, but if embraced, it can be every bit as fulfilling as even a great relationship.

A FINAL WORD FROM THE STOICS
'It is a much finer thing to be happy, to have a peaceful and undisturbed mind, to have what concerns you dependent on nobody but yourself.'
Epictetus, *Discourses*

RULE 36 Celebrate singledom

RULE 37
Embrace expert advice

'Advice is seldom welcome; and those who
want it the most always like it the least.'
Lord Chesterfield, *Letters to His Son*

WHEN YOU TELL a couples counsellor that your partner talks down to
you, and your partner responds with: 'It's called being condescending,
but you wouldn't know what that means,' then you are probably in the
right place.

Couples Therapy, an American TV show, is *Dr Phil* meets WWE, with
couples who storm off, talk over each other, stonewall and boil over in
anger. Naturally, as a review in *The Guardian* points out, a show such as
this does not reveal the long silences, refusal to speak, pregnant pauses
that stretch to infinity and silences that are heavy with regret and
frustration, because that would not make great telly. What it does reveal
is that a lack of sex is not only common but debilitating, and ultimately
proves fatal for many couples.

After a long, hard week of back-to-back meetings, school concerts
and an appointment to get a parent's hearing aid fine-tuned, there is
nothing like a couples counselling session where you rake over the state
of your relationship. This is where you sit side by side with your partner
or spouse, squirming as you listen to their laundry list of beefs they
have with you, such as how you interrupt them when they speak, how

you fritter away money on unnecessary items like a giant cat wheel, or how you're not romantic enough. Or conversely, you try to sugar-coat your own grievances with your other half, such as that they're 'not so generous-spirited with money', they reside 'somewhere near the mute end of the social spectrum', or they have 'the emotional insight of a gnat'. It is a brutal but necessary confessional that is about as appealing as stabbing your eyeballs, and yet with the right counsellor it can be transformative for some couples.

Finding a good counsellor is like finding a good relationship — it can take a lot of trial and error before you find someone you're both comfortable enough with to bare your souls to, and who can constructively navigate the relationship fissures that brought you there in the first place. You want someone who has the expertise to delicately shine a light on your differing perspectives and open up a new way of approaching the marital speedbumps that we all encounter. Some couples go to counselling for maintenance, others to see if they can repair a rupture, and still others when the end is nigh and they want to part gracefully, rather than in a fireball of contempt and recrimination. Usually, a counsellor will insist on no blame or shame, and will encourage the use of sentences starting with 'I feel' or 'I think', instead of sentences starting with 'you' — such as 'You always tell me off for forgetting the Kiev when I cook chicken Kiev.' The trick, counsellors advise, is to be curious, not judgemental.

Few of us are experts in human behaviour, and even those who are may struggle to examine their own relationships objectively. When a relationship has cracks running through it, counselling can help improve communication. If the cracks are too deep, then counselling might not necessarily bridge the chasm, but it might make a separation less fraught, and your future relationship with your ex more constructive.

What do the Stoics say?

There is nothing like a good splash of logic and reason to douse the flames of emotion that a counselling session can spark. Stoics value rationality and believe errors in judgement fuel destructive emotions. A calm and reasoned approach to an emotional situation is much more likely to help us proceed with wisdom and insight than hurling verbal grenades at our partner because we are wounded.

Epictetus encourages us to safeguard our reason. Just as we would avoid stepping on a nail, we should avoid inflicting damage on the highest faculties of our mind. He believed a life of wisdom was one of reason and clear thinking rather than faulty logic. Living wisdom rather than simply knowing it is more valuable.

A counselling session is meant to be about listening, and a good therapist will encourage this with exercises such as 'active listening'. This echoes Zeno's observation (which we met earlier) that we should adjust the ratio of talking to listening in line with our ratio of mouths to ears. Active listening involves listening to the other speak and then repeating back what they have said in our own words. It's remarkable how difficult this can be when emotions are running high, but it's a simple and powerful technique that helps us see the situation from the other's point of view, even if we don't agree with their perspective.

Epictetus added that we should mostly be silent and take things in, for 'there is a great danger in immediately throwing out what you have not digested'.

A FINAL WORD FROM THE STOICS

'To retract or mend a fault at the admonition of a friend in no way hurts your liberty.'
Marcus Aurelius, *Meditations*

RULE 37 Embrace expert advice

RULE 38
Let love go with grace

> 'Heaven hath no rage, like love to hatred turned,
> Nor Hell a fury, like a woman scorned.'
> William Congreve, *The Mourning Bride*

THERE IS NOTHING worse than trying to jump-start a relationship with someone who no longer cherishes you. (Obviously there are worse things, but this situation is not great.) Love needs to flow both ways to keep the ship afloat. If it slows to a trickle and the relationship is unable to be revived, then it is best to gracefully exit when the rupture is irreparable and the end is clearly nigh. Hemingway wrote in *A Farewell to Arms*: 'The world breaks everyone and afterward many are strong at the broken places.'

Some people take relationship endings well – like Gwyneth Paltrow and Chris Martin, who are famous for their 'conscious uncoupling'. Demi Moore and Bruce Willis, and Jennifer Aniston and Justin Theroux also reportedly had amicable divorces devoid of any mudslinging. High-school sweethearts Fran Drescher, of *The Nanny* fame, and Peter Marc Jacobson were together for more than 20 years before they split up. He came out as gay soon after, and she worked to support LGBTQ rights. Together, they made the show *Happily Divorced* and stayed best friends. 'Our love is unique, rare, and unconditional,' said Drescher, 'unless he's being annoying.'

Others handle the endings less well. Lucy took umbrage with her husband after he ended the marriage so he could move in with someone else. She cut up all his suits and keyed both sides of his car. Helen's reaction was less of anger and more of depression. She went out with friends and drowned her sorrows in alcohol. The next thing she remembered was waking up on a park bench with a possum feasting on a nearby vomit splatter, which she could only assume was her own. It was a low point.

Lisa busted her husband kissing her schoolfriend when she was putting the bins out. Turns out they had been having an affair for three months, so she left him and sold the family home. Her husband later discovered that Lisa had also been having an affair. Their marriage descended into a toxic separation. Yet with the passage of time, things softened, and amazingly they rebuilt a cordial post-break-up relationship.

The Road Less Traveled by psychiatrist M. Scott Peck is a masterclass in how to tackle difficulty and how to love. First up, he acknowledges that life is difficult, as accepting this reality lightens the burden. Complaining as though our struggles are uniquely unfair only accentuates our troubles. We can find meaning and opportunities for growth as we acknowledge and address problems in our relationships. Discipline is vital in the uncomfortable process of confronting and tackling difficult issues.

Peck offers some simple tools to help us confront pain: delay gratification, accept responsibility, and be dedicated to truth and balance. Those with the will to use these tools demonstrate true love. Some of us are hardwired to be optimistic — perhaps foolishly so — when confronted with difficult circumstances. Faced with calamity, it is a human condition to search for a silver lining to soften a harsh situation. Equally, our brains have a negativity bias in order to identify problems and be hyper-vigilant in response to things that might go wrong. The trick is to balance these forces and exit with dignity, rather than go down the bunny boiler route.

What do the Stoics say?

Epictetus provides an important perspective to take the heat out of a bust-up. He reminds us that love is mortal and as transient as the seasons. It would be foolish, he notes, to long for a fig or grape in the winter months.

In a major break-up, you will be faced with much that is outside of your control and with plenty of negativity. You will get emotional; this is natural. However, the Stoics taught us not to allow our emotions to take control of us. Externalising the emotion by viewing it as though it belongs to a third party allows us to distance ourselves from it, while still acknowledging and accepting it.

The Stoics wrote on the toxicity of negative emotions or 'passions', of which anger was one. For Seneca, 'Anyone enslaved to a passion is living under a tyrant.' Anger is a surface emotion reflecting an emotion below, such as hurt or rejection. It can be confusing and powerful but is rarely helpful. Seneca labelled it a 'frenzied madness'. This anger, if allowed to fester, can take control of your mind, leading to poor decisions. Your energy would better be poured into rebuilding your life than into fighting over assets and children.

To be angry and bitter after divorce is not inevitable. It is a choice made by at least one of the parties. You cannot dictate how your ex feels, but you do have power over your own emotions.

A FINAL WORD FROM THE STOICS

'It is essential that we not respond impulsively ... take a moment before reacting, and you will find it easier to maintain control.'

Epictetus, *Discourses*

RULE 38 Let love go with grace

RULE 39
Focus on the upside

'Divorce: the end of an error.'
Unknown

AFTER A BREAK-UP, there is an existential moment when you are in a flat, eating a ready-made vegetarian lasagne in front of the show *Below Deck* and you wonder: 'How did I get here? How did my life end up in marital breakdown, with all the complications of managing kids in a way that does not entirely screw up their lives? How did my decisions lead me to this moment?'

As we've seen, singledom is not always the curse we sometimes think. The upside of divorce is freedom, possibility and unpredictability. The freedom to watch comfort films like *Back to the Future* and *Raiders of the Lost Ark* whenever you feel like it. The freedom to wear a purple fluffy dressing gown at 5 pm and eat a Toblerone for dinner when the kids are with your ex.

The idea of divorce can percolate in your mind for a while. You think about the prospect with fear when your marriage hits choppy waters. When it comes, you might feel like a failure. You look at other couples walking breezily down the street and yearn to be like them.

The disappointment that life is not like a Richard Scarry book is part of living. The journalist and writer Nora Ephron said she remembered the pain of divorce but forgot the love. Of course, a divorce can last longer than a marriage, especially when there are children to consider. Ben went through an ugly divorce after his wife left him for another man, culminating in her secretly moving their children to another city. Once the kids had grown up and the pain of separation had subsided, a new set of dynamics emerged when grandchildren came into the picture. Ben and his ex-wife were almost having a tug-of-war over their toddler grandkids.

Putting your ex in the deep freeze, withholding critical parenting information, undermining the other parent to the kids, playing funny buggers with family finances or not pulling your weight by contributing to the family's costs are all examples of poor post-divorce behaviour. Instead, why not aim to be the best divorcee we possibly can be?

Change is painful, as anyone who has endured a corporate restructure can attest. But there is light at the end of the tunnel. And fun to be had. There may even be unexpected benefits: a nicer, more respectful relationship with your ex could emerge from the ashes.

A recently divorced friend went to a Christmas party, and an acquaintance she had known for years through their children drunkenly admonished her for leaving her lovely husband, 'who had done nothing wrong' – and how could she also leave her lovely kids? My friend explained that she hadn't left the children, but did not see the value in divulging the details of the marital breakdown. She did leave the conversation quickly to find a stiff drink and a more sympathetic friend. Just because a drunken person at a party has foot-in-mouth disease does not mean it needs to be contagious.

In extreme circumstances, a bad break-up might lead to chronic stress, or possibly even 'broken heart syndrome', which is medically known as takotsubo cardiomyopathy. This is where there is a sudden weakening of the heart, which leads to a rush of adrenaline that can shut down the heart's main pumping chamber. If only to avoid this affliction, it is worth cushioning the effects of a break-up on your health, regardless of who initiated the separation.

RULE 39 Focus on the upside

Amid the claims and counterclaims, we would all do well to remember the Buddhist phrase that 'no one saves us but ourselves. No one can and no one may. We ourselves must walk the path.' The road to divorce is commonly strewn with recriminations, finger pointing, tragedy, anxiety, sadness and, for some (unfairly), societal disapproval. A fortunate few experience none of these. In the end, we must all forge our own path.

What do the Stoics say?

If you are going through a messy bust-up, it is advisable to keep 'head-tilters' out of your orbit. Also ignore anyone who starts a sentence with the phrase 'You should'. This is a time of reinvention, when you are rebuilding your relationship with those friends and family you wish to spend time with. Those who are inconvenienced by the state of affairs might have strident opinions about what has happened, how poor your decision-making has been and what you must do next. Rarely mentioned is your own wellbeing.

Marcus Aurelius advised that we respond with compassion, not rage, when we believe we have been wronged, and that we recognise we are all flawed. Suffering comes from failing to appreciate our true nature and interconnectedness with others. The logos that governs our true nature causes no harm. As we've explored, these difficulties are opportunities to strengthen our soul.

A FINAL WORD FROM THE STOICS
'Every morning ... it will be your luck to meet some busybody, with some ungrateful, abusive fellow, with some knavish, envious, or unsociable churl or other.'
Marcus Aurelius, *Meditations*

RULE 40
Resist foot-in-mouth disease

'Dontopedalogy is the science of opening your mouth and putting your foot in it ... which I've practised for ... many years.'
Prince Philip, speech to the General Dental Council

WHEN SOMEONE YOU know is going through a separation or divorce, here are some tips on what *not* to say:

- 'What's wrong with you?'
- 'It's for the best.'
- 'I should divorce my husband, because ...'
- 'I should divorce my wife, because ...'
- 'You have to get back together.'
- 'We're still your friend.' (And then never call.)
- 'Have you thought about counselling?'
- 'How could you leave your lovely wife/husband/partner?'
- 'How could you do that to your kids?'
- 'How could you break up your family?'
- 'Why did they leave you?'
- 'Do you think it's menopause?'
- 'Do you think it's a midlife crisis?'
- 'Is your husband/wife/partner available?'
- 'I always thought your partner was hot.'

- 'I always thought you could do better.'
- 'I'm going to set you up with my brother's friend.'
- 'It's too early to move on.'
- 'I never liked your partner.'
- 'Are you on the dating apps?'
- 'Congratulations!'
- 'I'd rather be friends with your ex.'
- 'This has been hard on me.'
- 'Are you sure you know what you're doing?'
- 'It's going to be a shitstorm.'
- 'Why don't you get back with your ex, because you seem to get along?'
- 'You obviously enjoy separation because you've really drawn it out.'

The right things to say are pretty simple, really:

- 'How are things?'
- 'Do you want to catch up?'
- 'You'll get through this.'

You can also talk about anything else but the break-up, or share other people's horror stories. Perversely, this really can help.

What do the Stoics say?

It's difficult when someone close to you is in pain because of a break-up. Perhaps you loved their ex, perhaps you hated them, or maybe you didn't really know them at all. You will have your own life experiences to draw on, and these will taint your view of events. You may be desperate to give your opinion because of the impact this will have on you, or just because you really want to help. So it can be difficult to get the balance right between being a soundless cipher who offers nothing, and the opposite – someone who controls the conversation, dishing out advice and solutions.

Anyone who has been through a tough break-up will have encountered both extremes and a lot in between. The Stoics would encourage listening actively, entering the mind of the speaker and trying to truly understand their perspective. Only if we've done that are we likely to say the right thing. Sometimes that may be nothing at all. On other days it might be helpful to talk about other subjects, or to give sage and thoughtful advice. Channel the Stoic virtues of judgement and wisdom to know what to say and when to say it. If you feel that you're lacking in that department, the old adage applies: 'If in doubt, say nowt.'

A FINAL WORD FROM THE STOICS

'Accustom yourself to attend carefully to what is said by another, and as much as it is possible, be in the speaker's mind.'

Marcus Aurelius, *Meditations*

RULE 40 Resist foot-in-mouth disease

RULE 41
Minimise guilt and remorse

**'If you make it a habit not to blame others,
you will feel the growth of the ability to love
in your soul, and you will see the growth
of goodness in your life.'**
Leo Tolstoy, *A Calendar of Wisdom*

IN THE FILM *The Heartbreak Kid*, the main character, played by actor Ben Stiller, impulsively marries someone he believes to be the perfect woman, until she becomes an annoying lunatic who sings along to songs on the radio loudly off-key and has a septum affliction that means food spews out of her nostrils during meals.

Realising he's made a mistake, he goes for a walk along the beach during their honeymoon and stumbles across another woman he believes to be the love of his life. 'I made a huge mistake, okay?' he tells her family. 'Guilty. Boom. I stepped in it, big-time. And I admit it, okay? I jumped into a marriage way too quickly. I only knew my wife for a couple of months before we got married.'

The story reaches a climax when his spouse wees on him to relieve a jellyfish sting as his new girlfriend looks on and realises her beloved is married to another woman. He is suffering a bad case of guilt when he is unable to explain the full story to either woman. We in the audience wallow in our own guilt, because we feel empathy for this man as he ditches his wife on their honeymoon to pursue someone else.

Whoever ends a relationship might cop flak for calling time on the partnership. But often it takes more courage to end a relationship than to endure it miserably. Although it is horrific being dumped, at least the dumpee gets the benefit of feeling self-righteous – at least until everyone gets sick of hearing about what an a-hole their ex is.

Leo Tolstoy wrote a short story in 1909 titled 'There Are No Guilty People', although it was incomplete when he died. He also explored guilt and remorse in *Anna Karenina*: at one point the titular character says: 'Life is too short to hold grudges. Forgive and move on,' concluding that 'in the end, all that matters is how well you have loved, how well you have lived'. The book explores themes of life, death, betrayal, remorse and how the fear of dying without ever having loved is worse than the fear of death itself.

Dante's *Inferno* has a library of sins categorised in nine degrees of culpability, leaving a traitor who succumbs to lust in a worse state than a treacherous person. Those in the highest circles, however, are not remorseful – they may regret their circumstances, but not the adultery that sent them down to hell. Remorse cuts deeper, evoking a more profound regret, genuine empathy and insight into the consequences of an action that causes harm. Guilt is concentrated more on the act itself, as opposed to the impact and the pain inflicted on others.

What do the Stoics say?

According to Stoicism, focusing on the present is far preferable to dwelling on the past actions that made you feel guilty. Guilt falls into the same bucket as shame, regret, embarrassment and pride – none of which positively serve us as humans. They are a waste of precious time, because they focus on past actions that cannot be changed. The best you can do is not repeat the past behaviour or replicate whatever triggered the guilt in the first place.

When we compromise our values or hurt someone, either deliberately or unwittingly, we feel guilty. The person who ends the relationship cannot possibly carry all the guilt for the difficulties you both encountered. In most cases (obviously not all), a decline in affection and connection is the responsibility of both parties. If one partner wants out, then it would be unfair for the other to be kept in the dark about their misgivings.

The Stoics would focus on improving our own actions — including by being honest — rather than dwelling on outcomes that are beyond our control. Actions might include apologising, being more sympathetic, understanding that you cannot control another person's emotions, and being kind. Focusing on the present moment and practising forgiveness and compassion are more useful than wallowing in guilt.

A FINAL WORD FROM THE STOICS

'Those who are dedicated to a life of wisdom understand that the impulse to blame something or someone is foolishness.'

Epictetus (quoted in Lebell, *The Art of Living*)

RULE 42
Look after your pets

'The more one gets to know of men,
the more one values dogs.'
Alphonse Toussenel, *L'esprit des bêtes*

AMANDA AND DOUGLAS owned dogs, cats, gerbils and fish, and their menagerie expanded over the years as their children pushed them to acquire more animals. When the children got older and moved out, all that was left were the pets, who became the focus of communication. The couple sent each other photos of the fish, discussed how the dogs rolled in mud and let the cats nuzzle them overnight. Soon the dogs, Nessie and Bilbo, became their main companions, and they walked them alone instead of with their partner. On one of those walks, Amanda met her next husband, and the dogs, cats, gerbil and fish became collateral damage. Douglas moved out and Amanda stopped feeding the fish, which became floating carcasses, a metaphor for the end of the marriage (and a sad and unfair ending for the innocent fish). The pets were shuffled back and forth; the gerbil, apparently, died of a broken heart.

However, the cats and dogs became a lifeline of communication for Amanda and Douglas. The only messages the couple shared were over whose turn it was to walk the dogs and their custody arrangements over the holidays. Eventually, Amanda got the dogs while Douglas got the cats as he was alone and worked full-time. When they met up, the animals sensed the tension and jumped on their lap to soothe the raw emotions of the moment. Ever so gradually, it was those conversations and those meetings on the doorsteps with dog leads that restored civility.

Managing the custody of pets is difficult but necessary, and if splitting their time between two houses is in their best interests, then so be it. They have done the heavy lifting looking after everyone else's emotional wellbeing and need the best care arrangement possible.

As Nora Ephron said: 'When your children are teenagers, it's important to have a dog so that someone in the house is happy to see you.' But do remember, at the height of your emotion and suffering, that pets do need feeding – no killing the fish out of spite. Animals are portals of unconditional love and light, so not feeding them to spite your partner is an act of treachery. Look after your pets and they will look after you.

What do the Stoics say?

Seneca observed that animals don't wallow and hold onto sorrow like we do. Animals suffer pain and misery – they miss their owners when they're absent – but they are able to adapt and live in the moment. The dog whose owners are warring can show each of them love as though nothing has happened. In the misery of separation, with all its calls on long memories of a better time, or hopes for a better future, animals can remind us that there is only now. We should stay in the present moment as much as possible, showing love and care for one another.

The poet Walt Whitman was strongly influenced by Stoic philosophy. He reflects in his poem 'Animals' on their ability to live in the present and to reflect what he brings to them:

> I think I could turn and live with animals, they are so placid
> and self-contain'd,
> I stand and look at them long and long.

They do not sweat and whine about their condition,
They do not lie awake in the dark and weep for their sins,
They do not make me sick discussing their duty to God,
Not one is dissatisfied, not one is demented with the mania of
    owning things,
Not one kneels to another, nor to his kind that lived thousands
    of years ago,
Not one is respectable or unhappy over the whole earth.

So they show their relations to me and I accept them,
They bring me tokens of myself, they evince them plainly in
    their possession.

I wonder where they get those tokens,
Did I pass that way huge times ago and negligently drop them?

*Showing unconditional love to intelligent animals can create a loving
bond that the animals fully reciprocate with their own love.*

A FINAL WORD FROM THE STOICS

'Nor does any creature sorrow long for its offspring
except man – he nurses his grief, and the measure of
his affliction is not what he feels, but what he wills
to feel.'
Seneca, *To Marcia on Consolation*

RULE 42 Look after your pets

RULE 43
Keep your kids in the loop

**'Literature is mostly about having sex
and not much about having children.
Life is the other way round.'**
David Lodge, *The British Museum Is Falling Down*

THE MOST REMARKABLE thing about children is their adaptability.
One minute you think you have completely ruined their lives by
separating from their other parent, and that they'll flunk school,
become a drug dealer, and end up in juvenile detention and not liking
you too much. Next thing you know, they're laughing with their mates
playing Xbox, excelling at school and telling you that everything will
be okay like some wise oracle.

Children are incredibly resilient creatures. Without doubt, they can
bounce back and continue on the path they were on before a parental
break-up. It's important, though, to keep them informed about any
significant changes, while reassuring them of the things that will not
change: parents who love them, their school routine and their favourite
activities. They adjust course and continue with their lives.

Kids' resilience hinges on the ability of a separating couple,
firstly, not to trash one another, and, secondly, to maintain a unified
approach to parenting. That includes sharing vital information about
their lives so both parents can perform their duties, unless there are

safety reasons not to do so. Of course, if the absence of parental unity is what fuelled the break-up in the first place, then post-divorce parenting can be challenging. But the benefits for children of their parents maintaining a cordial relationship after splitting up cannot be overstated. However, sometimes circumstances make this impossible.

Despite your best efforts, an ocean of parental guilt can wash over you. You might feel like a failure, worrying that you have been unable to provide your kids with a fully functioning family unit. You might also lose a lot of access to them, depending on the parenting arrangements you reach with your ex.

This sense of dissatisfaction is accentuated by every interaction with parents who are still together. They say thoughtless things like 'I should divorce my husband – he keeps leaving the toilet seat up' or 'I'm so sick of my kids being around me the whole time'. That's why it can be bliss talking to parents who are in a similar boat to you. They understand that you lose those incidental moments with your children, and that time with them needs to be planned. That can be difficult when they are unresponsive teens who would rather hang out with their mates.

Much as we love our offspring on a cellular level (when they are nice to us), children place pressure on relationships. Articles on 'the 20 steps to a happy relationship' often begin with 'Don't have kids'. As David Lodge sagely observes, real life is more about kids and less about sex, the opposite of the stories we read in literature. Sure, children suck your time, money and freedom. But they also supply us with light and love – that is, if you can ignore the stench of rotten apple cores in your teenager's bedroom, or the worrying code of secrecy they operate under when you ask how their day was and get a one-word response: 'Fine.'

We are biologically programmed to worry constantly about our kids' happiness, safety, fulfilment and survival, and all that worry must slice years off our lives – and, for some couples, years off their relationship. A study from Princeton and Stony Brook universities found that life

RULE 43 Keep your kids in the loop

without children is more stable – there are, of course, fewer of the highs and lows associated with parenting. The happiness bump from having a baby has all but faded after a year. Over time, people without kids become happier compared to parents who are under the constant pressure of childrearing.

However, there is light. Happiness levels return when children have moved out of home, by which time the drama of parenting arrangements post-separation will have subsided. Until the grandchildren arrive – but that's another book.

What do the Stoics say?

Meredith Kunz, author of The Stoic Mom *blog, writes that Stoic parenting philosophy focuses on becoming more rational and mindful, and less anxious and controlling as parents, and giving our children more autonomy, especially as they get older. Parenting is intrinsically messy and we're going to make mistakes along the way, but if we do our best to make sound judgements, and they see us doing this, we are on the way to creating rounded human beings.*

A key judgement is what to share and not share with children. Keeping them informed of developments they need to know about is key, while not rubbishing an ex – even if they are rubbishing you. If possible, messaging to children should be consistent (assuming you are communicating with your ex), and key messages explained in age-appropriate ways. Ultimately, take comfort in the fact that children are frequently more resilient than their parents.

A FINAL WORD FROM THE STOICS

'For what makes a child? Want of knowledge. What makes a child? Want of instruction. For so far as a child knows those things he is no worse off than we are.'
Epictetus, *Discourses*

RULE 44
Move on

'What we call the beginning is often the end
And to make an end is to make a beginning.
The end is where we start from.'
T.S. Eliot, 'Little Gidding'

IF COUPLES MOVED on from one another at the same pace, then separation would be nothing more than a mild administrative blip. Perhaps that's an understatement, but it would definitely make life easier. But they do not, and hence the whole process is fraught.

In most cases, one member of the couple is psychologically several steps ahead of the other, having grieved the decline of the relationship before it officially concluded. This often means the other party is shocked, stagnant and bathed in grief. Friends have told me stories about recriminations: a push to ban one partner from the family home, threats to curtail child access, the withholding of information critical for the family, or the siphoning of money from joint accounts. Basically, all the behaviour you do not expect when you vow to love your spouse through thick and thin.

Wallowing in a sea of disbelief and despair after a break-up is to be expected. This is the phase where you cry on friends' shoulders over a glass (or a vat) of wine while streaming *Sleepless in Seattle* and *The First Wives Club* in your flannelette cat pyjamas and eating family-size blocks of chocolate. It's important to give yourself time to adjust to your new reality sans your life partner. Friend networks are crucial in providing support and uplifting your spirits. But if you're still in your pyjamas every Friday night, having put on 20 kilos after six months of binge-eating cheese and ice cream, the self-pity must come to an end. An extended period of wallowing may drive away friends and thwart any potential new romance.

The rule of thumb seems to be to allow for a year or two of self-reflection, growth and recovery before moving on. Remove reminders of the relationship, keep busy to avoid negative rumination, rely on a support network (including pets), don't bad-mouth your ex, and view the next phase of your life as a growth opportunity. This phase does not come to a hard stop, however – the heat slowly diminishes to the point where you can build a post-marital relationship, all going well. But some people refuse to move on, swimming in a sea of resentment, injustice, misery and despair. It may take them longer to accept their new reality, or they may never manage that.

If you're the kind of person who wants to disappear into the night and be done with the whole thing, good luck. Separation is a protracted process that would test the patience of a Buddhist monk. Very wealthy individuals like the supermodel Gisele Bündchen can slap down US$11.5 million on a waterfront mansion in Florida before a divorce is finalised to accelerate the process, but for the rest of us it travels at a snail's pace.

What do the Stoics say?

The Stoics never allowed themselves to become prisoners of their past, as the past cannot be altered in any way. Marcus Aurelius endured an incredible amount of change through his life, both as a father and as a ruler. 'Frightened of change?' he wrote. 'But what can exist without it? What's closer to nature's heart?' Change is inevitable. Some of it will be good, some bad. Our task is to navigate through the change that assails us, while also attempting to improve the world around us.

RULE 44 Move on

Epictetus — who, let's remember, was a slave for his first 30 years, and so endured incredible hardship — emphasised that the present time is all we have. 'Say rather, "Enable my mind to adapt itself to the issue, whatever it may be,"' he wrote.

Of course, moving on means making peace in our heart with our ex, while acknowledging that we can't control their thoughts or emotions. Epictetus said that when someone hurts us, we should say to ourselves, 'If I were that person and had endured the same trials, borne the same heartbreaks, had the same parents and so on, I probably would have done or said the same thing.'

Whether we've been left or we do the leaving, putting ourselves into the shoes of our ex in this way can help us heal. The benefit of this is as much for us as it is for those around us; it unshackles us from the slavery of regret and guilt, allowing us to become a free person once again.

A FINAL WORD FROM THE STOICS

Riches I hold in light esteem;
    And Love I laugh to scorn;
And lust of fame was but a dream
    That vanished with the morn:

And if I pray, the only prayer
    That moves my lips for me
Is, 'Leave the heart that now I bear,
    And give me liberty!'

Yes, as my swift days near their goal,
    'Tis all that I implore;
In life and death a chainless soul,
    With courage to endure.

Emily Brontë, 'The Old Stoic'

RULE 45
Don't give up on love

'Tis better to have loved and lost
Than never to have loved at all.'

Alfred, Lord Tennyson, 'In Memoriam A.H.H.'

SOMETIMES, WHEN A relationship falters, we can wonder whether love is dead. If even Hugh Jackman and his wife Deborra-Lee Furness couldn't make it, what hope is there for the rest of us? On the upside, their separation has placed Hugh back in the dating pool. Only I don't love Hugh. I love Simon Le Bon, the lead singer of Duran Duran (who is, annoyingly, married to Yasmin).

Maintaining optimism can help soften the anxiety we feel that we might not find love again. Looking on the bright side in response to pain and suffering is hardwired in our brains. That's why we persist in the search for love despite experiencing setbacks.

Some years ago, I went to a speed-dating event for people aged 39–59. It was held at a bar with polished cement floors, pendant lighting and a palpable atmosphere of loneliness. I wanted to see how an orchestrated event could lead to random love. The company that organised the night dazzled us with some impressive, if spurious, statistics to convince us that this was the right forum for finding our match. It promised that its unique algorithmic matching would result in 95 per cent of attendees dating someone they find attractive.

They claimed that more than one in four dates resulted in a five-star mutual match (though we were not told what 'five-star' actually meant). And that, over the course of the night, there was a 49 per cent chance of making at least one match.

When we all arrived, we were handed a champagne and offered salmon hors d'oeuvres and mini spinach quiches. We had eight minutes with eight potential matches. One man I met who was closer to 39 than 59 grumbled that we were all too old – but in my view, no woman, whatever their age, would have touched him with a barge pole, given his utter lack of joie de vivre. When the bell rang, another man appeared who was tall, handsome and swarthy. He was an arborist who lived with his labrador and boasted about having only one fork, one spoon and one knife in his house. Unsurprisingly, he too failed to woo any women.

Next up, a new-age bloke with hair down to his waist and sleeve tattoos sat down, closed his eyes and meditated. We sat in awkward silence until he opened his eyes, took a deep breath and said he had a message for me 'from the other side'. The message was that there would be no love tonight. Even without his spiritual insight, I could have told him that.

If anything, though, the event left me feeling positive and hopeful. I was more conscious of the randomness of love, of letting things, events and people percolate until they were just the right temperature for love. And it did, several times over, when I least expected it and from the unlikeliest of sources. For me, lowering my expectations created space from which love could spring forth.

What do the Stoics say?

Whether you're dusting yourself off after a string of questionable dates, a relationship that is treading water or one that has ended, we would all do well to consider Marcus Aurelius's enigmatic wisdom concerning enduring obstacles: 'The impediment to action advances action.

What stands in the way becomes the way.' The Roman emperor endured his fair share of difficulties in marriage, family and his work. Setbacks, Marcus believed, strengthen our soul.

This is the perfect mindset to bring to our quest for love — from the flutters of an early romance, to the stability of a long-term relationship, and finally to the train wreck of a break-up in which you are overcome by the need to listen to Radiohead on repeat. We must dust ourselves off, because a messy break-up that makes us wonder if love is deceased is in fact a lesson in resilience, humility and courage. And each heartbreak is a stepping stone towards finding a kindred spirit.

A FINAL WORD FROM THE STOICS
'If you wish to be loved, love.'
Seneca (quoting Hecato), 'On Philosophy and Friendship'

RULE 45 Don't give up on love

CONCLUSION

TO LOVE IS to risk loss, because love, like life, is transient. And weathering the dating merry-go-round requires the Stoic virtues of courage, patience and temperance. Once we find love, in all its magnificence, it can transform us into the best version of ourselves and hence be addictive. However, we must accept its impermanence. Sometimes our changing seasons align with our partners', and we rediscover the magic that first brought us together. Other times we outgrow one another. When things founder, it is hard to see through the quagmire of emotion that there is light at the end of the tunnel, and that love is not a finite resource.

Louise Erdrich, in her novel *The Painted Drum*, writes that love is our purpose on Earth. Risking our hearts and letting love swallow us up is the reason for our existence.

Before even worrying about whether love decays, we must find it in the first place, and that means wading through a field of unsuitable candidates. To do this requires patience and courage. The Stoics encouraged us to not leap to judgement, and to instead consider the perspectives of others. And also to expect to encounter meddlesome, troublesome and annoying people – good advice for those on the dating apps.

Once we find a prospective partner, it is best not to be a slave to our desires. And preferably refrain from leaving toenail clippings on the couch. Dealing with arguments before we go to sleep keeps things running smoothly. The Stoics supported cooperation and collaboration, and doing things purposely to achieve a goal, whether it is having a family, building wealth or course-correcting a relationship.

Our thoughts are within our control and shape our perception of reality. The Stoic framework brings rational thinking to the wild emotional roller-coaster of love. Self-reflection, inner calm and careful judgements help quell the firestorm of emotions. Difficulties strengthen our soul.

But the real test comes when love fades and succumbs to the weighty responsibilities of life. We are forced to confront the cold reality of life without our partner despite our expectations of happily-ever-after. Do we do a *Fatal Attraction* and torment our ex? Take the high road and build a post-relationship partnership that supports us to co-parent effectively? Or cut them loose and vanish?

The world subsists on change, and recognising the difference between a shift in circumstance and the emotion it stirs helps us better manage endings. The Stoics meditated on death because they knew that, ultimately, we are all going to die. Instead of allowing trivialities to consume us, we can use what precious time we have to love more.

ACKNOWLEDGEMENTS

THANK YOU AGAIN to Henry and Finny for being wonderful, lovable sons on the cusp of adulthood – the world is a richer place for having you both in it. You are both very much loved, and may you find the most exquisite, healthy and soul-nourishing love in your relationships. (However, I will be vetting from the sidelines.)

Thank you to Anthony Congedo, not only for supporting this book but for endorsing it on the front cover with great humour and for unearthing from primary sources such pertinent and insightful anecdotes. Not many exes would be so stoic and good-humoured in supporting a book about relationships while in the midst of a separation. Rebuilding our relationship in such a child-focused manner has been an incredible achievement and the opposite of many anecdotes explored in this book.

Thank you to all the Murdoch Books team – this feels like the Justice League regrouping for another instalment of Stoic wisdom. Jane Willson is a publisher extraordinaire, whose insights, wisdom and guidance are unfailingly brilliant. I will always be grateful for you putting faith in my book ideas. And to editorial manager Justin Wolfers, who has again been wonderful, accommodating and delightful to work with, and made me yearn for this to be a full-time gig. Once again, I had the privilege of working with editor Julian Welch, who embodies the Stoic virtues of patience and courage in his ability to lift and smooth out the prose, as well as wade through the never-ending footnotes.

I'm so grateful that Oslo Davis agreed once again to elevate the book with his hilarious illustrations, including the brilliant front cover. Thank you to Kristy Allen and Josh Durham for their superb book and cover design, which they nailed with few iterations. Thank you to Sarah Hatton and Maddy Boyling for your tireless media and marketing support.

And thank you to all my other exes throughout the decades – and a shout-out to my first boyfriend, Peter, for being such a good entrée into the world of love. Together, we saw live gigs including Nirvana, the Beastie Boys and Soundgarden, travelled to Byron Bay in a Kombi van and accidentally set fire to the ivy at one of our house parties. All my exes – some good, some not and others deeply incompatible – taught me a lot about love, and the sum of these lessons has helped me understand the kind of love that works best for me.

My sincere gratitude to all my friends who shared their hilarious past romantic mishaps and ingredients that help a relationship endure. A shout-out to Kate Arnott for gathering anecdotes from her friends, whose honesty was also greatly appreciated. (I promise I changed all your names!) Thank you to my generous, eagle-eyed family and friends – Mum, Serena, Sam, Eva and Fliss – for doing a final read through of the book before publication.

Thank you to my parents and family, who first introduced me to the concept of love, something they showed me (mostly) unconditionally. Yoshi and Boo have been two vital sources of love in recent times as a late-in-life crazy cat lady. Thank you to my divine network of friends (current and ex-journalists, St Kilda Primary School mums, Laurie chicks, university and work friends, and my lovely platonic male mates, including the Triangle of Tremendousness), whom I will cherish until the end of time.

Finally, another big, heartfelt thank you to my partner in crime, Dunstan Power, who saw my visible alarm at the extreme deadline for this book and pitched in to gather hilarious anecdotes (including the upside-down gnome and Dumping Dave), write and edit significant chunks, track down sources and quotes, and support me throughout the process. Your insights and perspectives on the subject of love were invaluable, and I'm grateful to have such a thoroughly lovely and lovable human in my orbit. The trick is for us all to channel some of this love into the wider world, which sorely needs a big hug. #youarethewindbeneathmywings

Acknowledgements

NOTES

I HAVE RELIED on the following sources for translations from the ancient Stoics:

John W. Basore, *De Brevitate Vitae—On the Shortness of Life* (Loeb Classical Library, William Heinemann, London, 1932)

Elizabeth Carter, *The Enchiridion by Epictetus* (S. Richardson, London, 1758)

Jeremy Collier, *The Meditations of Marcus Aurelius* (George Routledge & Sons, London, 1894)

A.S.L. Farquharson, *The Meditations of the Emperor Marcus Antoninus* (Clarendon Press, Oxford, 1944)

Richard M. Gummere, *Seneca: Ad Lucilium Epistulae Morales* (Loeb Classical Library, William Heinemann, London, 1917-1925)

Gregory Hays, *Meditations* (The Modern Library, New York, 2002)

Roger L'Estrange, *Seneca's Morals of a Happy Life, Benefits, Anger and Clemency* (Belford, Clarke & Co., Chicago, 1882)

George Long, *The Thoughts of the Emperor Marcus Aurelius Antoninus* (Little, Brown and Company, Boston, 1889)

P.E. Matheson, *The Discourses of Epictetus* (Clarendon Press, Oxford, 1916)

Aubrey Stewart, *Minor Dialogues, together with the Dialogue on Clemency* (G. Bell, London, 1889)

INTRODUCTION

'It is baffling that we …': This observation was inspired by Maria Popova, 'We Are the Music, We Are the Spark: Pioneering Biologist Ernest Everett Just on What Makes Life Alive', *The Marginalian*, 25 December 2023.

'The Rome of the love poems …': Charlotte Higgins, *Latin Love Lessons*, Short Books, London, 2007.

RULE 1

'As journalist Elle Hunt has noted …': Elle Hunt, '"The Longest Relationship of My Life': 10 Years of Dating through My Phone', *The Guardian*, 25 January 2024.

'According to the BBC …': BBC, 'The Science of Flirting', 17 September 2014, www.bbc.co.uk/science/hottopics/love/flirting.shtml.

'The Roman census …': Sabine R. Huebner, '"Brother-Sister" Marriage in Roman Egypt: A Curiosity of Humankind or a Widespread Family Strategy?', *Journal of Roman Studies*, vol. 97, 2007, pp. 21–49.

'If day and night your soul keeps …': Seneca, *Moral Letters to Lucilius*, Letter LIX (Gummere).

'But having determined in your mind …': Epictetus, *Enchiridion*, 32 (Matheson).

RULE 2

'When you imagine some pleasure …': Epictetus, *Enchiridion*, 34 (Matheson).

'without any anxious dependence …': Seneca, *Of a Happy Life, and Wherein It Consists*, Chapter 1 (L'Estrange).

'The great blessings of mankind …': Seneca, *Of a Happy Life, and Wherein It Consists*, Chapter 1 (L'Estrange).

RULE 3

'The chief task in life …': Epictetus, *Discourses*, 2.5 (Matheson).

'Not to feel exasperated …': Marcus Aurelius, *Meditations*, 5.9 (Hays).

RULE 4

'Psychotherapist and author Philippa Perry …': Philippa Perry, 'My Partner Ogles Other Women and It Makes Me Feel Unattractive', *The Guardian*, 7 April 2024.

'A woman in Canada …': Paul Farrell, 'Sonja Semyonova, 45, Claims She Is in an "Erotic" Relationship with an OAK TREE – after Feeling a "Connection" while Lying on Top of It during Lonely Covid Walks', *Daily Mail Australia*, 27 December 2023.

'All these things happen to them …': Marcus Aurelius, *Meditations*, 2.1 (Long).

'If anyone tells you …': Epictetus, *Enchiridion*, 33 (Carter).

RULE 5

'able both to abstain from …': Marcus Aurelius, *Meditations*, 1.16 (Long).

'Seneca viewed drunkenness …': Seneca, *Moral Letters to Lucilius*, Letter LXXXIII (Gummere).

'If it is good for you to drink …': Epictetus, *Discourses*, 3.14 (Matheson).

'When men have wearied themselves …': Seneca, *Moral Letters to Lucilius*, Letter LXXXIII (Gummere).

RULE 6

'Accustom yourself to give careful attention …': Marcus Aurelius, *Meditations*, 6.53 (Long).

RULE 7

'Philosopher Jonny Thompson has proposed …': Jonny Thomson, 'Mathematicians Suggest the "37% Rule" for Your Life's Biggest Decisions', *Big Think*, 21 April 2022.

'According to research published in *Nature* …': M. A. Addicott et al., 'A Primer on Foraging and the Explore/Exploit Trade-Off for Psychiatry Research', *Neuropsychopharmacology*, vol. 42, 2017, 1931–39.

'Let no-one enter who does not know mathematics': Bernard Suzanne, 'Frequently Asked Questions about Plato', 4 January 2004, www.dialogues-de-platon.org/faq/faq009.htm.

'If it is day, it is light …': Susanne Bobzien, 'Logic: The Stoics', in Keimpe Algra (ed.), *The Cambridge History of Hellenistic Philosophy*, Cambridge University Press, 1999.

'Reason, however, is surely the governing element …': Seneca, *Moral Letters to Lucilius*, Letter CXXIV (Gummere).

STOIC IN LOVE

RULE 8

'A Korean concept called *In-Yun* …': Jayfisherking, 'In-Yun: The Korean Concept of Cosmic Balance', *The Avalon Point*, 9 September 2023.

'harsh and invincible is her power …': Seneca, *De Consolatione ad Marciam*, quoted in 'From Divine Nature to Lady Fortune', *Modern Stoicism*, 11 February 2013.

'For the soul is more powerful': Seneca, *Moral Letters to Lucilius*, Letter XCVIII (Gummere).

RULE 9

'A man who had ghosted his live-in girlfriend …': Alison Green, 'I Ghosted My Ex, and She's About to Be My New Boss', *Ask a Manager*, 22 August 2017.

'Everything has two handles …': Epictetus, *Enchiridion*, 43 (Matheson).

RULE 10

'A 48-year-old lawyer from Estonia …': Stephen Gibbs, 'I'm 48 and I'm Head over Heels in Love with My Grandfather's 103-year-old Widow. Our 55-year Age Gap Is Irrelevant and Our Romance Has Nothing to Do with My Australian Visa Application', *Daily Mail Australia*, 1 February 2024.

'A Bumble survey of about 25,000 daters …': Bumble, 'What Will Dating Look Like in 2024? Here's What Bumble's Data Says', *The Buzz*, n.d.

'The new culture of pleasure and sophistication …': Charlotte Higgins, *Latin Love Lessons*, Short Books, London, 2007, p. 14.

'You should not copy the bad …': Seneca, *Moral Letters to Lucilius*, Letter VII (Gummere).

'Never regard something as doing you good …': Marcus Aurelius, *Meditations*, 3.7 (Hays).

'First tell yourself what kind of person …': Epictetus, *Discourses*, 3.23 (Matheson).

RULE 11

'We suffer more often in imagination than in reality …': Seneca, *Moral Letters to Lucilius*, Letter I (Gummere).

'It is a ridiculous thing …': Marcus Aurelius, *Meditations*, 7.71 (Long).

Notes

RULE 12

'Dear self …': Jay Shetty, *8 Rules of Love: How to Find It, Keep It, and Let it Go*, Thorsons, London, 2023.

'The wise man should rely …': Ruth Rothaus Caston, 'Love as Illness: Poets and Philosophers on Romantic Love', *Classical Journal*, vol. 101, no. 3, 2006, pp. 271–98.

'Avoid the many, avoid the few …': Seneca, *Moral Letters to Lucilius*, Letter X (Gummere).

RULE 13

'good relationships are built on several non-negotiable pillars …': Abigail Brenner, '5 Ways to Tell That Your Partner Is the Right One', *Psychology Today Australia*, 22 November 2020.

'Don't dream of what you don't already possess …': David Fideler, *Breakfast with Seneca: A Stoic Guide to the Art of Living*, W.W. Norton & Company, New York, 2022, p. 194.

'Hasten, therefore, in order that …': Seneca, *Moral Letters to Lucilius*, Letter XXXV (Gummere).

RULE 14

'We mortals have been endowed …': Seneca, *Moral Letters to Lucilius*, Letter CXVI (Gummere).

'It is not that we have …': Seneca, *On the Shortness of Life*, Chapter 1 (Basore).

'Even the storm, before it gathers': Seneca, *Moral Letters to Lucilius*, Letter CIII (Gummere).

RULE 15

'Dr Christian Jarrett, who used to edit …': Christian Jarrett, 'How Your Looks Shape Your Personality', *BBC Future*, 21 June 2019.

'repellent attire, unkempt hair, slovenly beard …': Seneca, *Moral Letters to Lucilius*, Letter V (Gummere).

'for a cultivated man to work hard …': Seneca, *Moral Letters to Lucilius*, Letter XV (Gummere).

'That which is really beautiful …': Marcus Aurelius, *Meditations*, 4.20 (Long).

RULE 16

'There are mental and physical benefits …': Francine Toder, 'Doing Absolutely Nothing Has Mental Health Benefits', *Psychology Today*, 23 July 2022.

'Be not heavy in business …': Marcus Aurelius, *Meditations*, 8.51 (Collier).

RULE 17

'Love languages, Gary Chapman says …': Gary Chapman, *The 5 Love Languages: The Secret to Love That Lasts*, Moody Publishers, Chicago, 2014.

'Society can only remain healthy …': Fideler, *Breakfast with Seneca*.

'There is not a man who …': Seneca, *Moral Letters to Lucilius*, Letter LXXXI (Gummere).

RULE 18

'An ABC article reports that love bombing …': Tahnee Jash, '"Love Bombing" Explained and Signs That Say Someone Is Genuinely Interested in You', *ABC Everyday*, 11 April 2022.

'Where things appear most plausible …': Marcus Aurelius, *Meditations*, 6.13 (Collier).

'When you imagine some pleasure …': Epictetus, *Enchiridion*, 34 (Matheson).

RULE 19

'One way to iron out any wrinkles …': Sarah Walker, '30 Lies Most Couples Live With', *MSN*, 16 December 2023.

'Questions might be …': See Sadie Whitelocks, 'Are You REALLY Ready to Tie the Knot? Psychologists Reveal the 12 Questions You Should Ask Your Partner Before Getting Married to Ensure You're Truly Meant to Be', *Daily Mail Australia*, 17 January 2023.

'Showing gratitude and appreciation for small things …': Dee Salmin, 'What You Need to Know About Moving In with Your Partner for the First Time', *ABC*, 23 February 2023.

'Stoics agreed that there were exceptions …': Marcelo Boeri, 'Review of *Arius Didymus. Epitome of Stoic Ethics. Texts and Translations 44; Graeco-Roman 14*', *Bryn Mawr Classical Review*, 2000.02.37.

'You have seen those things …': Marcus Aurelius, *Meditations*, 4.26 (Farquharson).

Notes

RULE 20

'One's own mind is a place ...': Marcus Aurelius, *Meditations*, 4.3 (Collier).

RULE 21

'Australian author Clementine Ford ...': Clementine Ford, *I Don't: The Case Against Marriage*, Allen & Unwin, Crows Nest, 2023.

'They supported radical egalitarianism ...': Fideler, p. 94.

'You ... should remind yourself ...': Epictetus, *Discourses*, 3.24 (Matheson).

RULE 22

'In May 1955, *Housekeeping Monthly* published ...': Angel Chang, 'This 1955 "Good House Wife's Guide" Tells How to Treat Husbands', *Little Things*, 19 February 2024.

'Speculation that her husband ...': Jessica Taylor & Bridie Pearson-Jones, 'Pictures that Rocked Danish Royalty: Crown Prince Frederik of Denmark and Mexican Socialite Genoveva Casanova's Night Out in Madrid without his Wife Princess Mary', *Daily Mail Australia*, 15 November 2023.

'Interestingly, married couples in a crowd ...': Karmela Padavic-Callaghan, 'Couples Collide with Fewer People on Walks than Pairs of Friends Do', *New Scientist*, 10 June 2023.

'A Purdue University team ...': Libby Richards, Melissa Franks and Rosie Shrout, 'Marriage Provides Health Benefits – and Here's Why', *The Conversation*, 14 January 2023.

'It is not right to reject the man ...': Catullus, Poem 62.

'Nature produced us related to one another ...': Seneca, *Moral Letters to Lucilius*, Letter XCV (Gummere).

'There are three relations ...': Marcus Aurelius, *Meditations*, 8.27 (Farquharson).

RULE 23

'Danish existentialist philosopher Søren Kierkegaard ...': Arthur C. Brooks, 'Kierkegaard's Three Ways to Live More Fully', *The Atlantic*, 11 January 2024.

'happiness and contentment are the DNA of pleasure ...': Robin Sharma, *The Greatness Guide: One of the World's Top Success Coaches Shares His Secrets for Personal and Business Mastery*, HarperCollins, New York, 2006.

'Boredom differs from comfort …': Kendra Cherry, 'What It Means if You're Bored in Your Relationship', *Verywell Mind*, 21 March 2023.

'seek pleasures of all kinds in all directions …': Seneca, *Moral Letters to Lucilius*, Letter LIX (Gummere).

'The wise man is joyful …': Seneca, *Moral Letters to Lucilius*, Letter LXIX (Gummere).

RULE 24

'Of all existing things …': Epictetus, *Enchiridion*, 1 (Matheson).

'The sum of the matter is this': Marcus Aurelius, *Meditations*, 4.26 (Farquharson).

RULE 25

'Stephanie Yates-Anyabwile, a family marriage therapist …': Stephanie Yates-Anyabwile, 'Therapist Breaks Down Couples Fighting in Movies & TV', *GQ*, 1 June 2021.

'He brands disagreements as "loose threads" …': Alain de Botton, *The Course of Love*, Penguin, London, 2016.

'American psychologist John Gottman …': Kyle Benson, 'The Magic Relationship Ratio, According to Science', The Gottman Institute, n.d.

'I begin to speak only when I'm certain …': Plutarch, *Cato the Elder*, 4.

'We shouldn't control our anger …': Seneca, *Of Anger*, 3.42 (Stewart).

'fog that shrouds the mind …': Seneca, *Of Anger*, 3.27 (Stewart).

'Remember that foul words or blows in themselves …': Epictetus, *Enchiridion*, 20 (Matheson).

RULE 26

'A 2023 study …': Indiana University, 'Married Couples Who Merge Finances May Be Happier, Stay Together Longer', *Science Daily*, 4 May 2023.

'And what is freedom, you ask? …': Seneca, *Moral Letters to Lucilius*, Letter LI (Gummere).

RULE 27

'Worse is calling your partner "babe"': Jen Doll, 'I Got You, Sweetikin: Why We Call Each Other Babe', *The Cut*, 4 December 2014.

'He once had Manilius …': Plutarch, *Lives*, vol. II, 17.7.

Notes

'The Greeks were similarly down ...': See Peter Walcot, 'Plutarch on Sex',
Greece & Rome, vol. 45, no. 2, 1998, pp. 166–87.

'Don't be prideful with any excellence ...': Epictetus, *Enchiridion*, 6 (Carter).

RULE 28

'Never have we expected more ...': Esther Perel, 'Meet Esther', 2023,
www.estherperel.com/about.

'Don't ask one person to give you ...': Esther Perel, 'Does Your Partner Expect
Too Much from You?', www.facebook.com/share/v/dTxPbJB1ZHjHmXHi.

'Remember: you shouldn't be ...': Marcus Aurelius, *Meditations*, 8.15 (Hays).

'It is great folly not to part ...': Marcus Aurelius, *Meditations*, 7.71 (Collier).

RULE 29

'Critical is how we repair cracks ...': Logan Ury, 'Want to Improve Your
Relationship? Start Paying More Attention to Bids', The Gottman Institute.

'If you really want to live on the edge ...': Nicole Rose Whitaker, 'Your
Personality, Explained by Your Annoying Household Habits', *The New
Yorker*, 16 February 2022.

'Never trust a Gary ...': Meghana Indurti & Tyler Fowler, 'Relationship Advice
from Your Aunt Who Has Been Divorced Six Times', *The New Yorker*, 3 March
2022.

'It is difficulties that show what men are': Epictetus, *Discourses*, 1.24
(Matheson).

'Valor withers without adversity': Seneca, *Of Providence*, II (Stewart).

'A recent study by Harvard researchers ...': Meredith Kunz, 'Stoic-Style Coping:
New Research', *The Stoic Gym*, n.d.

'Ask not that events should happen as you will ...': Epictetus, *Enchiridion*,
8 (Matheson).

RULE 30

'Humanist psychologist Scott Barry Kaufman ...': Rebecca Seal, 'The Healthy
Guide to Being Selfish: "It's OK to Not Meet Other People's Needs"', *The
Guardian*, 30 December 2023.

'The Universe, too, loves to create what is to be ...': Marcus Aurelius,
Meditations, 10.21 (Farquharson).

RULE 31

'Righteousness cannot be born …': Bertrand Russell, *Justice in War-Time*, Open Court, London, 1916, p. 192.

'Let me keep my distance …': Mary Oliver, 'Mysteries, Yes', 2009, see https://readalittlepoetry.com/2018/03/17/mysteries-yes-by-mary-oliver.

'the need to control often manifests …': Sharon Martin, 'How to Stop Being Controlling', *Psychology Today*, 3 March 2021.

'separate from yourself …': Marcus Aurelius, *Meditations*, 12.3 (Farquharson).

'What is done to me is ordained by nature …': Marcus Aurelius, *Meditations*, 5.25 (Hays).

'Don't regard what anyone says of you …': Epictetus, *Enchiridion*, 50 (Carter).

RULE 32

'The great sex drought has even hit …': 'The French Sex Recession: Has La Flamme Really Gone Out?', *The Guardian*, 8 February 2024.

'One sure-fire way of keeping …': Coco Khan, 'Men, Pick Up Your Toilet Brushes! It Could Solve the Great British Baby Shortage', *The Guardian*, 23 January 2024.

'in both France and Norway men tend to do more …': Yukiko Amano & Kyo Kitazume, 'To Raise Japan's Tepid Birthrate, Get Men Off the Couch', *Nikkei Asia*, 7 October 2021.

'Early Stoics such as Zeno and Chrysippus …': Diogenes Laertius, 'Zeno', *Lives of the Philosophers*.

'We receive comfort, even at a distance …': Seneca, *The Contents of a Happy Life*, XVIII (L'Estrange).

RULE 33

'About 60 per cent of men …': Kerri Sackville, 'Why Are We Still Shocked by Infidelity? Most of Us Cheat', *The Sydney Morning Herald*, 30 September 2022.

'British actress Amy Nuttall …': Simon Boyle, 'TOUGH NUTT: Emmerdale Star Amy Nuttall Is BACK With Love Rat Husband and Issues Seven Rules He Must Obey', *The Sun*, 3 July 2023.

'Infidelity at the tail end …': Billie Schwab Dunn, 'Are You Being Unfaithful

Without Even Realising? Psychologist Explains Why Micro-cheating Is on the Rise – and How to Spot a Cheater', *Daily Mail Australia*, 11 January 2018.

'A healthy relationship is unlikely to emerge ...': Catherine Shuttleworth, 'New Study Identifies Patterns that Lead to Infidelity in Long-term Relationships', *Indy 100*, 29 November 2023.

'The Stoics did not agree ...': Massimo Pigliucci, 'Infidelity: A Stoic's Perspective', *IAI News*, 16 February 2018.

'The Roman poet Horace tells ...': Horace, *Satires*, 1.2.31–5.

'avoid impurity to the upmost ...': Epictetus, *Enchiridion*, 33 (Matheson).

'An active sex life ...': Epictetus, *Enchiridion*, 33 (Matheson).

'If laying aside that fidelity': John Bonforte, *The Philosophy of Epictetus*, Philosophical Library, New York, 1955, p. 96.

RULE 34

'Amazingly, 10–15 per cent ...': Ann Gold Buscho, 'Why Divorced Partners End Up Remarrying Each Other', *Psychology Today*, 7 June 2022.

'a new venture between two experienced co-founders ...': Arthur C. Brooks, 'Why the Most Successful Marriages Are Start-Ups, Not Mergers', *The Atlantic*, 12 October 2023.

'You must plan your life ...': Marcus Aurelius, *Meditations*, 8.32 (Farquharson).

RULE 35

'Pigeons may have a brain the size of a bean ...': Brandon Keim, 'What Pigeons Teach Us about Love', *Nautilus*, 4 February 2016.

'The universe is change ...': Marcus Aurelius, *Meditations*, 4.3.

'the chief test of all ...': Epictetus, *Enchiridion*, 1 (Matheson).

'Two elements must therefore be rooted out ...': Seneca, *Moral Letters to Lucilius*, Letter LXXVIII (Gummere).

RULE 36

'for of what benefit is a quiet neighbourhood ...': Seneca, *Moral Letters to Lucilius*, Letter LVI (Gummere).

'Men seek retreats for themselves ...' Marcus Aurelius, *Meditations*, 4.1 (Long).

'It is a much finer thing to be happy ...': Epictetus, *Discourses*, 4.36 (Matheson).

RULE 37

'*Couples Therapy*, an American TV show …': Lucy Cavendish, 'I've Seen Everything as a Counsellor. But *Couples Therapy* Still Has Me Gripped', *The Guardian*, 22 January 2022.

'To retract or mend a fault …': Marcus Aurelius, *Meditations*, 8.16 (Collier).

RULE 38

'The world breaks everyone …': Ernest Hemingway, *A Farewell to Arms*, Scribner, New York, 1929, p. 216.

'First up, he acknowledges …', M. Scott Peck, *The Road Less Traveled: A New Psychology of Love, Traditional Values, and Spiritual Growth*, Simon & Schuster, New York, 1978.

'Anyone enslaved to a passion …': Seneca, *Of Anger*, Book III (translated by David Fideler).

'It is essential that we not respond impulsively …': Epictetus, *Discourses*, 3.23 (Matheson).

RULE 39

'Every morning …': Marcus Aurelius, *Meditations*, 2.1 (Collier).

RULE 40

'Accustom yourself to attend carefully …': Marcus Aurelius, *Meditations*, 6.53 (Long).

RULE 41

'Those who are dedicated …': Epictetus (translated by Sharon Lebell), *The Art of Living: The Classical Manual on Virtue, Happiness and Effectiveness*, HarperOne, New York, 1995, p. 11.

RULE 42

'The poet Walt Whitman was strongly influenced …': George Hutchinson, 'Stoicism', in J.R. LeMaster & Donald D. Kummings (eds), *Walt Whitman: An Encyclopedia*, Garland Publishing, New York, 1998.

'Nor does any creature sorrow long …': Seneca, *To Marcia on Consolation*, vi.3–vii.3.

Notes

RULE 43

'Don't have kids …': Rebecca Chant, 'The Happiest Relationships Have These
20 Things in Common', *Espresso*, 3 January 2024.

'A study from Princeton and Stony Brook universities …': Angus Deaton &
Arthur A. Stone, 'Evaluative and Hedonic Wellbeing among Those With
and Without Children at Home', *PNAS*, vol. 111, no. 4, 2014, pp. 1328–33.

'Happiness levels return …': Caitlin McCormack, '30 Signs Your Relationship
Won't Last', *Espresso*, 29 June 2023.

'For what makes a child? …': Epictetus, *Discourses*, 2.1 (Matheson).

RULE 44

'Frightened of change? …': Marcus Aurelius, *Meditations*, 7.18 (Hays).

'Say rather …': Epictetus, *Discourses*, 2.14 (Matheson).

'If I were that person …': Epictetus (translated by Sharon Lebell), *The Art
of Living: The Classical Manual on Virtue, Happiness and Effectiveness*,
HarperOne, 1995.

'Riches I hold in light esteem …': Emily Brontë, *The Complete Poems*, Penguin
Classics, New York, 1992.

RULE 45

'Maintaining optimism can help soften …': Deena Mousa, 'Why We Search for
Silver Linings', *Nautilus*, 13 March 2024.

'If you wish to be loved, love': Seneca, *Moral Letters to Lucilius*, Letter IX
(Gummere).

CONCLUSION

'Love is our purpose on earth …': Louise Erdrich, *The Painted Drum*,
HarperCollins, New York, 2009.

ANNIE LAWSON is a former journalist who has had a diverse love life, from kiss chasey in the school yard in primary school, to a first pash as a teenager with braces to several boyfriends including one who alphabetised cereal packets, and finally to marriage, which ended. This all taught her that the key to a good relationship is not only lots of storage, regular holidays at a nice resort and someone who is funny, but finding a partner to do nothing with. She now works as a business editor after a stint on the dark side of the corporate world and is a devoted student of the Stoics, taking every opportunity to apply their wisdom to life's hard things. Her bestselling first book, *Stoic at Work,* published in 2023, has been translated into six languages.
@annielawson_author

OSLO DAVIS is an illustrator and artist who makes lively, witty work for both his own amusement and for publications and projects worldwide.
oslodavis.com / @oslodavis

Murdoch Books Australia
Cammeraygal Country
83 Alexander Street, Crows Nest NSW 2065
Phone: +61 (0)2 8425 0100
murdochbooks.com.au
info@murdochbooks.com.au

Murdoch Books UK
Ormond House, 26–27 Boswell Street,
London WC1N 3JZ
Phone: +44 (0) 20 8785 5995
murdochbooks.co.uk
info@murdochbooks.co.uk

 A catalogue record for this book is available from the National Library of Australia

A catalogue record for this book is available from the British Library

ISBN 9 781 7615 004 04

Cover design by Design by Committee
Text design by Kristy Allen
Cover illustration by Oslo Davis

Typeset by Midland Typesetters
Printed and bound by CPI (UK) Ltd, Croydon CR0 4YY

We acknowledge that we meet and work on the traditional lands of the Cammeraygal people of the Eora Nation and pay our respects to their elders past, present and future.

10 9 8 7 6 5 4 3 2 1